Thinking through Sources
Exploring American Histories

Volume 2: Since 1865

Thinking through Sources
Exploring American Histories

Volume 2: Since 1865

Third Edition

Nancy A. Hewitt
Rutgers University

Steven F. Lawson
Rutgers University

bedford/st.martin's
Macmillan Learning
Boston | New York

For Bedford/St. Martin's

Vice President, Editorial, Macmillan Learning Humanities: Edwin Hill
Program Director for History: Michael Rosenberg
Senior Program Manager for History: William J. Lombardo
History Marketing Manager: Melissa Rodriguez
Director of Content Development: Jane Knetzger
Developmental Editor: Stephanie Sosa
Senior Content Project Manager: Gregory Erb
Assistant Content Project Manager: Natalie Jones
Senior Workflow Project Manager: Lisa McDowell
Production Supervisor: Robert Cherry
Media Project Manager: Sarah O'Connor
Media Editor: Mary P. Starowicz
Composition: Lumina Datamatics, Inc.
Text Permissions Manager: Kalina Ingham
Photo Permissions Editor: Christine Buese
Photo Researcher: Candice Cheesman
Director of Design, Content Management: Diana Blume
Text Design: Lumina Datamatics, Inc.
Cover Design: William Boardman
Cover Image: Front of St. Paul's Cathedral, Tremont St., c. 1936 (oil on board), Crite,
    Allan Rohan (1910–2007)/Boston Athenaeum, USA/Gift of the artist, 1971/
    Bridgeman Images
Printing and Binding: LSC Communications

Manufactured in the United States of America.

1   2   3   4   5   6   23   22   21   20   19   18

For information, write: Bedford/St. Martin's, 75 Arlington Street, Boston, MA 02116

ISBN 978-1-319-13230-9

Acknowledgments
*Text acknowledgments and copyrights appear at the back of the book on page 243, which
constitutes an extension of the copyright page. Art acknowledgments and copyrights appear
on the same page as the art selections they cover.*

PREFACE

"History," Mark Twain reputedly said, "doesn't repeat itself, but it does rhyme." While Twain was not suggesting that the past was poetry or the lyrics of a song, he did recognize that historical events create echoes that continue to resonate into the present. To hear and decipher those sounds across the centuries, scholars and students must listen carefully to the chorus of voices that, taken together, provide a soundtrack of American histories. Of course, not all voices rhyme perfectly with other voices, and there are also harsh and dissonant voices. The primary source projects in this reader allow us to hear many different sounds as we seek to interpret particular moments in the American past.

This reader for the third editions of *Exploring American Histories* and *Exploring American Histories,* Value Edition, consists of a series of primary source projects, each of which contains about five sources of different types from different viewpoints focused on a particular event, issue, or development at key points in U.S. history. The primary source projects follow the chapter structure of *Exploring American Histories* and are styled like the projects in the full version of the textbook. The sources include maps, personal letters and diaries, memoirs, advertisements, posters, cartoons, paintings, government reports, speeches, trial testimony, song lyrics, and laws. The roster of historical figures represented in these sources includes well-known individuals and organizations as well as ordinary women and men. The document projects range, for example, from "Mapping America" to "Home-Front Protest during the Civil War" in Volume 1 and from "Women in the West" to "The Environment and Federal Policy in the Twenty-First Century" in Volume 2. The project on "Reconstruction in South Carolina" appears in both volumes. Each project includes a central question, a brief introduction and headnotes to the primary sources, followed by five "Interpret the Evidence" questions and one or two "Put It in Context" questions. These questions encourage students to recognize connections among sources and relate the sources to larger historical themes. Students must also consider the range of sources, the quality of evidence in each source, and the relevance of that evidence to the questions and the larger context as they analyze the sources and build an interpretation.

The reader is available in both print and electronic formats and is built into the LaunchPad for *Exploring American Histories* so that you and your students can access the sources wherever and whenever it is convenient for you. If you choose to pair LaunchPad with your print books, students will have access to multiple-choice quizzes for the sources and our "Thinking through Sources" pedagogy, which consists of an auto-graded activity at the end of each project that asks students to make supportable inferences and draw appropriate conclusions from the sources. "Thinking through Sources" culminates in a set of essay questions that build upon the historical arguments students developed in the auto-graded activity. It is through reading and analyzing the sources that students will begin, as Mark Twain might have put it, to hear the rhymes of the past in the present.

GUIDE TO ANALYZING PRIMARY SOURCES

In their search for an improved understanding of the past, historians look for a variety of evidence — written sources, visual sources, and material artifacts. When they encounter any of these primary sources, historians ask certain key questions. You should ask these questions too. Sometimes historians cannot be certain about the answers, but they always ask the questions. Indeed, asking questions is the first step in writing history. Moreover, facts do not speak for themselves. It is the task of the historian to organize and interpret the facts in a reasoned and verifiable manner.

Analyzing a Written Primary Source

- What kind of source is this? For example, is it a diary, letter, speech, sermon, court opinion, newspaper article, witness testimony, poem, memoir, or advertisement?
- Who wrote the source? How can you identify the author? Was the source translated by someone other than the author or speaker (for example, American Indian speeches translated by whites)?
- When and where was it written?
- Why was the source written? Is there a clear purpose?
- Who was, or who might have been, its intended audience?
- What point of view does it reflect?
- What can the source tell us about the individual(s) who produced it and the society from which he, she, or they came?
- How might individuals' race, ethnicity, class, gender, and region have affected the viewpoints in the sources?
- In what ways does the larger historical context help you evaluate individual sources?

Analyzing a Visual or Material Primary Source

- What kind of visual or material source is this? For example, is it a map, drawing or engraving, physical object, painting, photograph, census record, or political cartoon?
- Who made the image or artifact, and how was it made?
- When and where was the image or artifact made?
- Can you determine if someone paid for or commissioned it? If so, how can you tell that it was paid for or commissioned?

- Who might have been the intended audience or user? Where might it have originally been displayed or used?
- What message or messages is it trying to convey?
- How might it be interpreted differently depending on who viewed or used it?
- What can the visual or material source tell us about the individual who produced it and the society from which he or she came?
- In what ways does the larger historical context help you evaluate individual sources?

Comparing Multiple Primary Sources

- In what ways are the sources similar in purpose and content? In what ways are they different?
- How much weight should one give to who wrote or produced the source?
- Were the sources written or produced at the same time or at different times? If they were produced at different times, does this account for any of the differences between or among the sources?
- What difference does it make that some sources (such as diaries and letters) were intended to be private and some sources (such as political cartoons and court opinions) were meant to be public?
- How do you account for different perspectives and conclusions? How might these be affected by the author's relative socioeconomic position or political power in the larger society?
- Is it possible to separate fact from personal opinion in the sources?
- Can the information in the sources under review be corroborated by other evidence? What other sources would you want to consult to confirm your conclusions?

Cautionary Advice for Interpreting Primary Sources

- A single source does not tell the whole story, and even multiple sources may not provide a complete account. Historians realize that not all evidence is recoverable.
- Sources have biases, whether they appear in personal or official accounts. Think of biases as particular points of view, and try to figure out how they influence the historical event and the accounts of that event.
- Sources reflect the period in which they were written or produced and must be evaluated within the historical time frame from which they came. Explain how people understood the world in which they lived, and be careful to avoid imposing contemporary standards on the past. Nevertheless, remember that even in any particular time period people disagreed over significant principles and practices such as slavery, imperialism, and immigration.
- Sources often conflict or contradict each other. Take into account all sides. Do not dismiss an account that does not fit into your interpretation; rather, explain why you are giving it less weight or how you are modifying your interpretation to conform to all the evidence.

CONTENTS

Reconstruction in South Carolina

▶ **Evaluate how African Americans and northern Republicans viewed Reconstruction in different and changing ways.**

South Carolina offers an interesting case study of the course of Reconstruction in the South following the Civil War. It was the first state to secede from the Union in 1860, and the majority of its population was black. By the war's end, blacks in South Carolina had already begun what the historian Willie Lee Rose called a "rehearsal for Reconstruction" by occupying the Sea Islands. Once the state reentered the Union, Republican voters elected black officials and even sent African American representatives to serve in Congress (Sources 14.1 and 14.3). It was the only state where blacks controlled the state legislature.

However, like the other southern states, South Carolina capitulated to white supremacy. The Ku Klux Klan maintained a campaign of terror (Source 14.5), and northern support for Reconstruction withered. Commentators like the artist Thomas Nast argued that African American elected officials were unfit for office. The federal government backed away from supporting reconstructed Republican governments, and white Democrats returned to power in South Carolina in 1877. Still, Reconstruction marked a significant, if short-lived, historical moment when African Americans participated in and led an interracial democracy.

The following primary sources offer an overview of key themes concerning Reconstruction in South Carolina.

SOURCE 14.1 | COLORED PEOPLE'S CONVENTION OF SOUTH CAROLINA, *Memorial to Congress* (1865)

After the Civil War, African Americans in South Carolina wasted no time in asserting their newfound rights as freedpeople. The Colored People's Convention of South Carolina met in November 1865 and presented the following list of demands to Congress.

Gentlemen:

We, the colored people of the State of South Carolina, in Convention assembled, respectfully present for your attention some prominent facts in relation to our present condition, and make a modest yet earnest appeal to your considerate judgment.

We, your memorialists, with profound gratitude to almighty God, recognize the great boon of freedom conferred upon us by the instrumentality of our late President, Abraham Lincoln, and the armies of the United States.

"The fixed decree, which not till Heaven can move,
Thou, Fate, fulfill it; and, ye Powers, approve."

We also recognize with liveliest gratitude the vast services of the Freedmen's Bureau together with the efforts of the good and wise throughout the land to raise up an oppressed and deeply injured people in the scale of civilized being, during the throbbings of a mighty revolution which must affect the future destiny of the world.

Conscious of the difficulties that surround our position, we would ask for no rights or privileges but such as rest upon the strong basis of justice and expediency, in view of the best interests of our entire country.

We ask first, that the strong arm of law and order be placed alike over the entire people of this State; that life and property be secured, and the laborer free to sell his labor as the merchant his goods.

We ask that a fair and impartial instruction be given to the pledges of the government to us concerning the land question.

We ask that the three great agents of civilized society—the school, the pulpit, the press—be as secure in South Carolina as in Massachusetts or Vermont.

We ask that equal suffrage be conferred upon us, in common with the white men of this State.

This we ask, because "all free governments derive their just powers from the consent of the governed"; and we are largely in the majority in this State, bearing for a long period the burden of onerous taxation, without a just representation. We ask for equal suffrage as a protection for the hostility evoked by our known faithfulness to our country and flag under all circumstances.

We ask that colored men shall not in every instance be tried by white men; and that neither by custom or enactment shall we be excluded from the jury box.

We ask that, inasmuch as the Constitution of the United States explicitly declares that the right to keep and bear arms shall not be infringed and the Constitution is the Supreme law of the land—that the late efforts of the Legislature of this State to pass an act to deprive us of arms be forbidden, as a plain violation of the Constitution, and unjust to many of us in the highest degree, who have been soldiers, and purchased our muskets from the United States Government when mustered out of service.

Source: James S. Allen, *Reconstruction: The Battle for Democracy, 1865–1876* (International Publishers, 1937), Appendix, 228–29.

We protest against any code of black laws the Legislature of this State may enact, and pray to be governed by the same laws that control other men. The right to assemble in peaceful convention, to discuss the political questions of the day; the right to enter upon all the avenues of agriculture, commerce, trade; to amass wealth by thrift and industry; the right to develop our whole being by all the appliances that belong to civilized society, cannot be questioned by any class of intelligent legislators.

We solemnly affirm and desire to live orderly and peacefully with all the people of this State; and commending this memorial to your considerate judgment.

Thus we ever pray.

SOURCE 14.2 | LOTTIE ROLLIN, *Address on Universal Suffrage* (1870)

For some black women in South Carolina, Reconstruction offered the opportunity to agitate for a true universal suffrage—one that included blacks and whites, women and men. Three African American sisters—Charlotte (Lottie), Frances, and Louisa Rollin—mobilized for voting rights. Lottie Rollin gave the following address at a women's rights convention in Columbia, South Carolina in 1870.

It had been so universally the custom to treat the idea of woman suffrage with ridicule and merriment that it becomes necessary in submitting the subject for earnest deliberation that we assure the gentlemen present that our claim is made honestly and seriously. We ask suffrage not as a favor, not as a privilege, but as a right based on the ground that we are human beings, and as such, entitled to all human rights. While we concede that woman's ennobling influence should be confined chiefly to home and society, we claim that public opinion has had a tendency to limit woman's sphere to too small a circle, and until woman has the right of representation this will last, and other rights will be held by an insecure tenure.

SOURCE 14.3 | ROBERT BROWN ELLIOTT, *In Defense of the Civil Rights Bill* (1874)

The English-born politician Robert Brown Elliott held a number of local and state offices in South Carolina during Reconstruction. He also became one of seven black members of the U.S. Congress when he won election to the House of Representatives in 1870. Elliott was a champion of black rights at each stage of his political career. On January 6, 1874, he gave the following address before Congress in defense of what would become the Civil Rights Act of 1875. In this excerpt, he counters Georgia senator Alexander Stephens's argument for states' rights.

Source: Elizabeth Cady Stanton, Susan B. Anthony, and Matilda Joslyn Gage, eds., *History of Woman Suffrage*, vol. 3, *1876–1885* (Rochester: Susan B. Anthony, 1886), 828.

Mr. Speaker:

While I am sincerely grateful for this high mark of courtesy that has been accorded to me by this House, it is a matter of regret to me that it is necessary at this day that I should rise in the presence of an American Congress to advocate a bill which simply asserts equal rights and equal public privileges for all classes of American citizens. I regret, sir, that the dark hue of my skin may lend a color to the imputation that I am controlled by motives personal to myself in my advocacy of this great measure of national justice. Sir, the motive that impels me is restricted by no such narrow boundary, but is as broad as your Constitution. I advocate it, sir, because it is right. The bill, however, not only appeals to your justice, but it demands a response from your gratitude.

In the events that led to the achievement of American independence the Negro was not an inactive or unconcerned spectator. He bore his part bravely upon many battlefields, although uncheered by that certain hope of political elevation which victory would secure to the white man. The tall granite shaft, which a grateful State has reared above its sons who fell in defending Fort Griswold against the attack of Benedict Arnold, bears the name of Jordan, Freeman, and other brave men of the African race, who there cemented with their blood the corner-stone of the Republic. In the State which I have the honor in part to represent (South Carolina) the rifle of the black man rang out against the troops of the British Crown in the darkest days of the American Revolution. Said General Greene, who has been justly termed the "Washington of the North," in a letter written by him to Alexander Hamilton, on the 10th of January, 1781, from the vicinity of Camden, South Carolina: "There is no such thing as national character or national sentiment. The inhabitants are numerous, but they would be rather formidable abroad than at home. There is a great spirit of enterprise among the black people, and those that come out as volunteers are not a little formidable to the enemy."

At the battle of New Orleans under the immortal Jackson, a colored regiment held the extreme right of the American line unflinchingly, and drove back the British column that pressed upon them at the point of the bayonet. . . .

But, sir, we are told by the distinguished gentleman from Georgia (Mr. Stephens) that Congress has no power under the Constitution to pass such a law, and that the passage of such an act is in direct contravention of the rights of the States. I cannot assent to any such proposition. The Constitution of a free government ought always to be construed in favor of human rights. Indeed, the thirteenth,

Source: Alice Moore Dunbar, ed., *Masterpieces of Negro Eloquence: The Best Speeches Delivered by the Negro from the Days of Slavery to the Present Time* (New York: The Bookery Publishing Company, 1914), 67–70, 81–82, 85–87.

fourteenth, and fifteenth amendments, in positive words, invest Congress with the power to protect the citizen in his civil and political rights. Now, sir, what are civil rights? Rights natural, modified by civil society. . . .

When, therefore, the honorable gentleman from Georgia lends his voice and influence to defeat this measure, I do not shrink from saying that it is not from him that the American House of Representatives should take lessons in matters touching human rights or the joint relations of the State and national governments. . . .

Sir, it is scarcely twelve years since that gentleman shocked the civilized world by announcing the birth of a government which rested on human slavery as its cornerstone. The progress of events has swept away that pseudo-government which rested on greed, pride, and tyranny; and the race whom he then ruthlessly spurned and trampled on is here to meet him in debate, and to demand that the rights which are enjoyed by its former oppressors — who vainly sought to overthrow a Government which they could not prostitute to the base uses of slavery — shall be accorded to those who even in the darkness of slavery kept their allegiance true to freedom and the Union. Sir, the gentleman from Georgia has learned much since 1861; but he is still a laggard. . . .

Technically, this bill is to decide upon the civil status of the colored American citizen; a point disputed at the very formation of our present form of government, when by a short-sighted policy, a policy repugnant to true republican government, one Negro counted as three-fifths of a man. The logical result of this mistake of the framers of the Constitution strengthened the cancer of slavery, which finally spread its poisonous tentacles over the southern portion of the body politic. To arrest its growth and save the nation we have passed through the harrowing operation of intestine war, dreaded at all times, resorted to at the last extremity, like the surgeon's knife, but absolutely necessary to extirpate the disease which threatened with the life of the nation the overthrow of civil and political liberty on this continent. In that dire extremity the members of the race which I have the honor in part to represent — the race which pleads for justice at your hands to-day, — forgetful of their inhuman and brutalizing servitude at the South, their degradation and ostracism at the North, flew willingly and gallantly to the support of the national Government.

Their sufferings, assistance, privations, and trials in the swamps and in the rice-fields, their valor on the land and on the sea, form a part of the ever-glorious record which makes up the history of a nation preserved, and might, should I urge the claim, incline you to respect and guarantee their rights and privileges as citizens of our common Republic. But I remember that valor, devotion, and loyalty are not always rewarded according to their just deserts, and that after the battle some who have borne the brunt of the fray may, through neglect or contempt, be assigned to a subordinate place, while the enemies in war may be preferred to the sufferers.

The results of the war, as seen in reconstruction, have settled forever the political status of my race. The passage of this bill will determine the civil status, not only of the Negro, but of any other class of citizens who may feel themselves discriminated against. It will form the cap-stone of that temple of liberty, begun on this continent under discouraging circumstances, carried on in spite of the sneers of monarchists and the cavils of pretended friends of freedom, until at last it stands, in all its beautiful symmetry and proportions, a building the grandest which the world has ever seen, realizing the most sanguine expectations and the highest hopes of those who, in the name of equal, impartial, and universal liberty, laid the foundation-stone.

SOURCE 14.4 | JAMES SHEPHERD PIKE,
The Prostrate State (1874)

Throughout the 1870s, some northern writers lost enthusiasm and faith in Reconstruction. James Shepherd Pike, a Maine Republican, had supported Radical Reconstruction. In 1874, however, he published *The Prostrate State*, in which he argued that Reconstruction in South Carolina had failed. In the following excerpt, Pike describes his thoughts on South Carolina's interracial government.

Here, then, is the outcome, the ripe, perfected fruit of the boasted civilization of the South, after two hundred years of experience. A white community, that had gradually risen from small beginnings, till it grew into wealth, culture, and refinement, and became accomplished in all the arts of civilization; that successfully asserted its resistance to a foreign tyranny by deeds of conspicuous valor, which achieved liberty and independence through the fire and tempest of civil war, and illustrated itself in the councils of the nation by orators and statesmen worthy of any age or nation — such a community is then reduced to this. It lies prostrate in the dust, ruled over by this strange conglomerate, gathered from the ranks of its own servile population. It is the spectacle of a society suddenly turned bottom-side up. The wealth, the intelligence, the culture, the wisdom of the State, have broken through the crust of that social volcano on which they were contentedly reposing, and have sunk out of sight, consumed by the subterranean fires they had with such temerity braved and defied.

In the place of this old aristocratic society stands the rude form of the most ignorant democracy that mankind ever saw, invested with the functions of government. It is the dregs of the population habilitated in the robes of

Source: James Shepherd Pike, *The Prostrate State: South Carolina under Negro Government* (New York: D. Appleton and Company, 1874), 11–15.

their intelligent predecessors, and asserting over them the rule of ignorance and corruption, through the inexorable machinery of a majority of numbers. It is barbarism overwhelming civilization by physical force. It is the slave rioting in the halls of his master, and putting that master under his feet. And, though it is done without malice and without vengeance, it is nevertheless none the less completely and absolutely done. Let us approach nearer and take a closer view. We will enter the House of Representatives. Here sit one hundred and twenty-four members. Of these, twenty-three are white men, representing the remains of the old civilization. These are good-looking, substantial citizens. They are men of weight and standing in the communities they represent. They are all from the hill country. The frosts of sixty and seventy winters whiten the heads of some among them. There they sit, grim and silent. They feel themselves to be but loose stones, thrown in to partially obstruct a current they are powerless to resist. . . .

Deducting the twenty-three members referred to, who comprise the entire strength of the opposition, we find one hundred and one remaining. Of this one hundred and one, ninety-four are colored, and seven are their white allies. Thus the blacks outnumber the whole body of whites in the House more than three to one. On the mere basis of numbers in the State the injustice of this disproportion is manifest, since the black population is relatively four to three of the whites. A just rectification of the disproportion, on the basis of population merely, would give fifty-four whites to seventy black members. And the line of race very nearly marks the line of hostile politics. As things stand, the body is almost literally a Black Parliament, and it is the only one on the face of the earth which is the representative of a white constituency and the professed exponent of an advanced type of modern civilization.

SOURCE 14.5 | HARPER'S WEEKLY, "Worse Than Slavery" *Political Cartoon* (1874)

The Ku Klux Klan and other white vigilante groups rose after the Civil War to overthrow African American political participation and preserve white supremacy and black subordination, as depicted in this *Harper's Weekly* cartoon from October 1874. Two years later, racial violence erupted in the small, all-black town of Hamburg, South Carolina. A black militia unit there clashed with whites from nearby communities, leading to the deaths of six blacks and one white. The Democratic Party used the so-called "Hamburg Massacre" to campaign successfully against "Republican Rule," which they claimed led to racial violence, and they regained political power in 1876.

How easily wicked and treasonable organizations may gain the control over the peaceable and the industrious members of society has always been signally apparent at the South. A | Tennessee, venture even to denounce the murderers or the violators of the laws; or if any Northern journal, roused to a proper indignation by the wrongs inflicted upon peaceable settlers

INTERPRET THE EVIDENCE

1. What did the Colored People's Convention of South Carolina demand in the months after the end of the war (Source 14.1)? How did the participants justify their arguments?

2. According to Lottie Rollin, why do women deserve the right to vote (Source 14.2)? How does she appeal to traditional gender norms in making this argument?

3. How does Robert Brown Elliott cite history in defense of the Civil Rights Bill (Source 14.3)? Why did blacks deserve the equal rights of citizenship? How does Elliott discredit Stephens's arguments?

4. According to James Shepherd Pike, what was wrong with South Carolina's government (Source 14.4)? How does he describe the black members of the South Carolina legislature? The white members?

5. What audience was "Worse than Slavery" (Source 14.5) aimed toward?

6. According to the Colored People's Convention, Rollin, and Elliott, what constituted equal citizenship for African Americans?

PUT IT IN CONTEXT

1. How does Pike's book show how Republicans in the North backed away from Reconstruction?

Women in the West

▶ Describe the challenges western women faced in the late nineteenth century and analyze how these challenges compared to those faced by men.

Women who migrated to the West at the end of the nineteenth century faced many challenges. Perhaps most obviously, the journey itself proved long, dangerous, and sometimes deadly for migrants and homesteaders. When they reached their destination, women and their families typically found scarcely better conditions. Life in the West was lonely and filled with grueling work. Women toiled as hard as, if not harder than, their husbands. Many immigrant women, particularly Chinese women in cities like San Francisco, found themselves locked into virtual slave conditions as prostitutes. And for the American Indian women already living in the West, the arrival of white migrants presented new difficulties (Source 15.3).

Yet life in the West also presented opportunities. Martha Jane "Calamity Jane" Cannary Burk (Source 15.1) embraced the adventure. Other women and men looked forward to the chance to start over and build new lives as well (Source 15.2). Life in the West also allowed some women to pursue reform causes. Women led temperance movements and successfully agitated for suffrage (Sources 15.4 and 15.5).

The following primary sources offer insight into the varied lives of women in the West.

SOURCE 15.1 | MARTHA JANE CANNARY BURK, *The Life and Adventures of Calamity Jane* (1896)

The exploits—real or imagined—of "Calamity Jane" exemplified the possibilities for adventure in the West. Martha Jane Cannary Burk worked as a scout and traveled extensively through the region. She fought Indians and became a friend of famed gunfighter Wild Bill Hickok. Her short autobiography of 1896 featured a number of embellishments about her life.

In 1865 we emigrated from our homes in Missouri by the overland route to Virginia City, Montana, taking five months to make the journey. While on the way the greater portion of my time was spent in hunting along with the men and hunters of the party, in fact I was at all times with the men when there was excitement and adventures to be had. By the time we reached Virginia City I was considered a remarkable good shot and a fearless rider for a girl of my age. I remember many occurrences on the journey from Missouri to Montana. Many times in crossing the mountains the conditions of the trail were so bad that we frequently had to lower the wagons over ledges by hand with ropes for they were so rough and rugged that horses were of no use. We also had many exciting times fording streams for many of the streams in our way were noted for quicksands and boggy places, where, unless we were very careful, we would have lost horses and all. Then we had many dangers to encounter in the way of streams swelling on account of heavy rains. On occasions of that kind the men would usually select the best places to cross the streams, myself on more than one occasion have mounted my pony and swam across the stream several times merely to amuse myself and have had many narrow escapes from having both myself and pony washed away to certain death, but as the pioneers of those days had plenty of courage we overcame all obstacles and reached Virginia City in safety.

Mother died at Black Foot, Montana, 1866, where we buried her. I left Montana in Spring of 1866, for Utah, arriving at Salt Lake city during the summer. Remained in Utah until 1867, where my father died, then went to Fort Bridger, Wyoming Territory, where we arrived May 1, 1868, then went to Piedmont, Wyoming, with U.P. Railway. Joined General Custer as a scout at Fort Russell, Wyoming, in 1870, and started for Arizona for the Indian Campaign. Up to this time I had always worn the costume of my sex. When I joined Custer I donned the uniform of a soldier. It was a bit awkward at first but I soon got to be perfectly at home in men's clothes.

Was in Arizona up to the winter of 1871 and during that time I had a great many adventures with the Indians, for as a scout I had a great many dangerous missions to perform and while I was in many close places always succeeded in getting away safely for by this time I was considered the most reckless and daring rider and one of the best shots in the western country.

After that campaign I returned to Fort Sanders, Wyoming, remained there until spring of 1872, when we were ordered out to the Muscle Shell or Nursey Pursey Indian outbreak. In that war Generals Custer, Miles, Terry and Crook were all engaged. This campaign lasted until fall of 1873.

It was during this campaign that I was christened Calamity Jane. It was on Goose Creek, Wyoming, where the town of Sheridan is now located. Capt. Egan was in command of the Post. We were ordered out to quell an uprising of the Indians, and were out for several days, had numerous skirmishes during which six of the soldiers were killed and several severely wounded. When on returning to the Post we were ambushed about a mile and a half from our destination. When

---

Source: Martha Cannary Burk, *The Life and Adventures of Calamity Jane* (Billings, MT, 1896), 1–3.

fired upon Capt. Egan was shot. I was riding in advance and on hearing the firing turned in my saddle and saw the Captain reeling in his saddle as though about to fall. I turned my horse and galloped back with all haste to his side and got there in time to catch him as he was falling. I lifted him onto my horse in front of me and succeeded in getting him safely to the Fort. Capt. Egan on recovering, laughingly said: "I name you Calamity Jane, the heroine of the plains." I have borne that name up to the present time.

SOURCE 15.2 | *Black Migrants to Kansas* (1880)

African American women also went West in significant numbers: 6,000 in the year 1879 alone. They and their families left the South in hopes of escaping white supremacy and racial violence. Most migrated to Kansas, where Benjamin "Pap" Singleton had promoted organizing new communities. In the following interviews conducted by Colonel Frank H. Fletcher, who was appointed to study African American migration to Kansas, several Kansas "Exodusters" reflect on their journey.

I give you the exact language of the colonists as written down by me at the time, thinking that their own expressions, although ungrammatical, will present more clearly the information sought.

NANCY GUPTIL: Came from Middle Tennessee. Heard neighbors talking of Kansas two or three years. We received two or three circulars that told about Kansas. I lived with a white man who took Kansas papers. There are not many such white men in the South. I find things here a heap better than I expected. We have forty acres. We came last May. We built our house in the fall. My husband finds enough work around here to support us. We had plenty of supplies to live on through the winter. We got them by working for white neighbors. Politics never pestered us at the South, but the people took all we made. People treats us better here than they did there, because they is willing to pay us what we work for. Before I came we had letters about this country from a son-in-law at Topeka. We have a prayer-meeting every Wednesday night, and every two weeks of a Sunday in my house. Am a Baptist. I wouldn't go back for nothing. Singleton lived in Nashville. All my people are mighty well satisfied here. . . .

MRS. WILLIAM RAY: Came from Texas in a wagon of our own; stopped a while at Fort Scott. We left Texas because they treated us so bad. They took out my husband's brother-in-law and shot him three times in the face. They came after my husband one night and made him give up his pistol. They took my aunts and son-in-law out and beat them. They struck my aunt and cut her, because she would not tell where her son was. We have been on this place between four and five years. We have a hundred and sixty acres. My husband

Source: Col. Frank H. Fletcher, *Negro Exodus: Report of Col. Frank H. Fletcher, Agent Appointed by the St. Louis Commission to Visit Kansas for the Purpose of Obtaining Information in Regard to Colored Emigration* (1880), 3–6.

hires help. [At this point the husband, who had been ploughing in an adjoining field with two other men, came up and continued the narration.] Last year I raised five hundred and sixty bushels of corn, fifty bushels of wheat, one hundred and sixty bushels of oats, two hundred and fifty bushels of potatoes. I sold fifteen dollars' worth of garden vegetables, one cow, ten hogs, four or five dollars' worth of chickens, six bushels of plums, three hundred pounds butter and two bushels of eggs. I have now seven horses, twenty hogs, and eight head of cattle. My children are learning to read and write. They go to the same school with the whites. We have church and Sunday-school in the schoolhouse. We are Baptists. . . .

MRS. CARTER: Came from Tennessee to St. Louis, and lived there three years. We thought when we left Tennessee that we would be furnished a horse and plow and a hundred and sixty acres. That story rushed up a great many. We heard there was plenty of land at Topeka. Singleton said we would have to pay for land. Hill said the Government would help us and find us something to eat. I think this is a very good country; none of the colored colonists have to beg for any thing they need. My husband gets all the work he can do. They pay him very well. I would scratch in the ground here before I would go back South. I have seen droves come in, that were run away from what they made down South. My husband could not get his money at all there.

SOURCE 15.3 | ZITKALA-ŠA (GERTRUDE BONNIN), *"Impressions of an Indian Childhood"* (1921)

Gertrude Simmons Bonnin, who later took the Indian name Zitkala-Ša, lived on the Yankton Reservation in South Dakota with her mother and brother until 1884, when missionaries recruited her to attend school so that she would become assimilated into Anglo-American culture. After attending a Quaker school in Wabash, Indiana, Zitkala-Ša briefly attended Earlham College and then taught at the Carlisle Indian Industrial School in Pennsylvania for two years. During that time, she experienced a reawakening of her American Indian heritage and consciousness, and in 1921 published the following account of her life on the Sioux reservation.

MY MOTHER

A WIGWAM of weather-stained canvas stood at the base of some irregularly ascending hills. A footpath wound its way gently down the sloping land till it reached the broad river bottom; creeping through the long swamp grasses that bent over it on either side, it came out on the edge of the Missouri.

Here, morning, noon, and evening, my mother came to draw water from the muddy stream for our household use. Always, when my mother started for the river, I stopped my play to run along with her. She was only of medium height.

Source: Zitkala-Ša (Gertrude Bonnin), *American Indian Stories* (Washington: Hayworth Publishing House, 1921). University of Pennsylvania Digital Library, "A Celebration of Women Writers." http://digital.library.upenn.edu/women/zitkala-sa/stories/stories.html#impressions

Often she was sad and silent, at which times her full arched lips were compressed into hard and bitter lines, and shadows fell under her black eyes. Then I clung to her hand and begged to know what made the tears fall.

"Hush; my little daughter must never talk about my tears"; and smiling through them, she patted my head and said, "Now let me see how fast you can run today." Whereupon I tore away at my highest possible speed, with my long black hair blowing in the breeze.

I was a wild little girl of seven. Loosely clad in a slip of brown buckskin, and light-footed with a pair of soft moccasins on my feet, I was as free as the wind that blew my hair, and no less spirited than a bounding deer. These were my mother's pride, – my wild freedom and overflowing spirits. She taught me no fear save that of intruding myself upon others. . . .

Returning from the river, I tugged beside my mother, with my hand upon the bucket I believed I was carrying. One time, on such a return, I remember a bit of conversation we had. My grown-up cousin, Warca-Ziwin (Sunflower), who was then seventeen, always went to the river alone for water for her mother. Their wigwam was not far from ours; and I saw her daily going to and from the river. I admired my cousin greatly. So I said: "Mother, when I am tall as my cousin Warca-Ziwin, you shall not have to come for water. I will do it for you."

With a strange tremor in her voice which I could not understand, she answered, "If the paleface does not take away from us the river we drink."

"Mother, who is this bad paleface?" I asked.

"My little daughter, he is a sham, – a sickly sham! The bronzed Dakota is the only real man."

I looked up into my mother's face while she spoke; and seeing her bite her lips, I knew she was unhappy. This aroused revenge in my small soul. Stamping my foot on the earth, I cried aloud, "I hate the paleface that makes my mother cry!"

Setting the pail of water on the ground, my mother stooped, and stretching her left hand out on the level with my eyes, she placed her other arm about me; she pointed to the hill where my uncle and my only sister lay buried.

"There is what the paleface has done! Since then your father too has been buried in a hill nearer the rising sun. We were once very happy. But the paleface has stolen our lands and driven us hither. Having defrauded us of our land, the paleface forced us away.

"Well, it happened on the day we moved camp that your sister and uncle were both very sick. Many others were ailing, but there seemed to be no help. We traveled many days and nights; not in the grand, happy way that we moved camp when I was a little girl, but we were driven, my child, driven like a herd of buffalo. With every step, your sister, who was not as large as you are now, shrieked with the painful jar until she was hoarse with crying. She grew more and more feverish. Her little hands and cheeks were burning hot. Her little lips were parched and dry, but she would not drink the water I gave her. Then I discovered that her throat was swollen and red. My poor child, how I cried with her because the Great Spirit had forgotten us!

"At last, when we reached this western country, on the first weary night your sister died. And soon your uncle died also, leaving a widow and an orphan daughter, your cousin Warca-Ziwin. Both your sister and uncle might have been happy with us today, had it not been for the heartless paleface."

My mother was silent the rest of the way to our wigwam. Though I saw no tears in her eyes, I knew that was because I was with her. She seldom wept before me.

SOURCE 15.4 | ABIGAIL SCOTT DUNIWAY, *Speaking Out for the Right to Vote* (1914)

Abigail Scott Duniway led the drive for women's suffrage in Oregon. Like many women activists of the time, she united the cause of women's suffrage with temperance, the movement to prohibit the use of alcohol. Duniway also distinguished herself as a writer and newspaper editor. The following excerpt from her autobiography describes her first visit to the Oregon legislature, during which she spoke in favor of a bill to grant Oregon women the right to vote.

I went to Salem in September, 1872, to visit the Legislature, which met annually at that time in the autumn, in a little brick building, across the street from the Chemeketa, now known as the Willamette Hotel. As no woman prior to that time had visited the Legislature, except occasionally with others, on some social occasion in honor of the success of some political aspirant, I found it difficult to prevail upon a woman to accompany me. As the etiquette of those times demanded that I must have a chaperone, I spent two whole days in canvassing the city in quest of a friend who would dare to escort me. The first woman in Oregon to undertake a mission so far out of the ordinary, was Dr. Mary P. Sawtelle, who was being widely criticized at that time, as the first Oregon woman to dare to graduate from any medical institution, and receive her diploma as a regular physician. This doctor, who had failed to pass "exams" as a "regular" at home, had but recently returned from an Eastern Medical Institute, fully equipped with the accessories of a physician's degree; and, being known as an active rebel against an early and most unfortunate domestic relation, which had married her off at the age of fifteen and compelled her to bear four children before she was twenty, was objected to, afterwards, as my chaperone, for the alleged reason that I should have selected a woman of whom their husbands, or a regular masculine doctor, had no cause to be jealous, or afraid. But Dr. Sawtelle's sad domestic experiences appealed to me, from the first, as the principal reason why I should defend her openly. She was then happily remarried, and was the pioneer pathbreaker among the great army of divorced women—servants without wages—whom District Judges, good and

Source: Abigail Scott Duniway, *Path Breaking: An Autobiographical History of the Equal Suffrage Movement in the Pacific Coast States* (Portland, OR: James, Kerns & Abbott Co., 1914), 59–61.

true, are now rescuing from legalized prostitution, through the machinery of the divorce court. . . .

When Dr. Sawtelle and I entered the legislative hall my heart thumped audibly, as I realized that I was entering a domain considered sacred to the aristocracy of sex. We took our seats in the lobby of the House of Representatives, where for a full minute I felt in danger of fainting and creating a scene. But Hon. Joseph Engle, perceiving the situation and knowing me personally, arose to his feet, and, after a complimentary speech, in which he was pleased to recognize my position as a farmer's wife, mother, home-maker, teacher and now as journalist, moved that I be invited to a seat within the bar and provided with table and stationery, as were the other members of the newspaper profession. The motion carried, with only two or three dissenting votes; and the way was open, from that time forward, for women to compete with men, on equal terms, for all minor positions in both branches of the Legislature—a privilege of which they have not been slow to take advantage. . . .

The late Hon. Samuel Corwin introduced a Woman Suffrage Bill in the House, early in the session; and while it was pending, I was invited to make an appeal in its behalf, of which I remember very little, so frightened and astonished was I, except that I once, inadvertently, alluded to a gentleman by his name, instead of his county, whereupon, being rapped to order, I blushed and begged pardon, but put myself at ease by informing the members that in all the bygone years, while they had been studying parliamentary rules, I had been rocking the cradle. One member who had made a vehement speech against the bill, in which he declared that no respectable woman in his county desired the elective franchise, became particularly incensed, as was natural, upon my exhibiting a woman suffrage petition from his county, signed by the women whom he had misrepresented, and headed by his own wife.

SOURCE 15.5 | CAROLINE NICHOLS CHURCHILL, *Fighting for Woman Suffrage in Colorado* (1909)

Caroline Nichols Churchill emerged as the key leader of the women's suffrage movement in Colorado. Like Duniway, Churchill published a newspaper, the *Colorado Antelope*. She fought for women's suffrage as the state experienced incredible labor strife. In the following excerpt from her memoir, which she wrote in the third person, Churchill reveals her politics, her personality, and the rifts within the women's suffrage movement.

Mrs. Churchill, with the help of some of the women from outside towns, called a convention. The city women, perhaps troubled because of their laurels, came in and were at once installed in the offices, thus giving experienced people a chance to at least make themselves useful as well as ornamental. Mrs. Churchill

Source: Caroline Nichols Churchill, *Active Footsteps* (Colorado Springs: Mrs. C. N. Churchill, 1909), 211–14.

steadfastly refused office, as the conducting of a paper in the interests of the cause was enough for any one head.

The convention adjourned with the best of feeling. The men's papers made all the capital they possibly could out of the fact that Mrs. Churchill was not given office, assuming that the honor of such a position would have been irresistible to any mortal woman with healthy ambition. Mrs. Churchill seems to have been created superior to such a thing as personal aggrandizement. What she wants is a civilization that will come somewhere near filling the wants of the great mass of the people. Federal control of schools; that general illiteracy from any cause may disappear from the world. The idea of holding children responsible for the bad management of those interested in ignorance and depravity, and those gone before, is repugnant to any fair-minded person. If women could be induced to perform their public duties, which would be to become a helpmeet for man in public affairs as in private matters, many things could be done that are now wholly neglected. The minds of such men as Chaucer and Ruskin have given this subject attention and have concluded that man will only cease being a marauder and a warrior when women do enough to teach them that there is nothing in the course usually pursued by the masculine portion of the human family. . . .

Mrs. Churchill was never popular with the W.C.T.U. [Woman's Christian Temperance Union], because popularity was not what she was looking for. A better condition of things was her watchword. Her methods were her own. She never tried to persecute any organization, or belittle them, because their methods were different from her own. One of the Anthony family, living at Leavenworth, Kas., once wrote to have Mrs. Churchill get interested in his business. Mrs. Churchill was fairly harassed by these importunities from different sources, and answered these letters rather saucily sometimes. Susan B. Anthony perhaps realized that there was younger blood in the field and may have thought her laurels in danger. When the brother failed to interest the new woman in his schemes, she had no further use for Mrs. Churchill and would show her resentment as opportunity made it possible. Lucy Stone exchanged papers with Mrs. Churchill for fourteen years, but in all that time never had a good word for Mrs. Churchill or her work. Mrs. Churchill thought the question for which she was giving her life work of more importance than self-aggrandizement.

INTERPRET THE EVIDENCE

1. What does Calamity Jane's autobiography indicate about the difficulties of traveling West (Source 15.1)? What does her work reveal about gender roles?

2. Why did the "Exodusters" move to Kansas (Source 15.2)? How did they feel about their decisions?

3. Compare the experiences of Zitkala-Ša and her mother (Source 15.3) with those of white and African American women in the West. How do you explain the differences?

4. How does Abigail Scott Duniway's story reveal the gender norms of western life and politics (Source 15.4)? How did Duniway mobilize these gender norms to further her own ends?

5. According to Caroline Nichols Churchill, what are the benefits of granting women the right to vote (Source 15.5)? What were her larger social and political goals? How does her memoir reveal conflicts among suffragists?

PUT IT IN CONTEXT

1. Why do you think women suffragists found success in the West before they did in the East?

Labor and Race in the New South

▶ Analyze how "new" the New South was compared to the "Old" South with respect to race and labor.

With the end of Reconstruction in 1877, the southern states returned to what whites called "home rule": the law of white supremacy. Democratic governments regained control in every southern state, and whites solidified their social, political, and economic power. By the early twentieth century, every southern state had passed Jim Crow laws that segregated and disfranchised blacks despite the promises of the Fourteenth and Fifteenth Amendments (Sources 16.4 and 16.5).

Yet some southern whites proclaimed that the South had in fact changed. They argued that a "New South," characterized by a modernizing, industrializing economy, would come to dominate the nation and the world (Source 16.1). They praised the end of slavery and promised a new era of racial cooperation—on whites' terms. Some changes did indeed occur, although not on the scale that New South boosters claimed. The South remained primarily agricultural. And African Americans found themselves subjugated as tenant farmers and sharecroppers, although they still valued their freedom and protested their discriminatory treatment (Source 16.3).

The following documents reveal the cleavages over labor and race in the New South.

SOURCE 16.1 | HENRY GRADY, *The New South* (1890)

No booster did more to spread the ideal of the New South than Henry Grady, editor of the *Atlanta Constitution*. Grady gave speeches across the country extolling the virtues of southern industry, as well as the relationship between whites and blacks in the aftermath of Reconstruction. The following excerpts from his 1890 book, *The New South*, expand on these ideas.

A few years ago I told, in a speech, of a burial in Pickens county, Georgia. The grave was dug through solid marble, but the marble headstone came from Vermont. It was in a pine wilderness, but the pine coffin came from Cincinnati. An iron mountain overshadowed it, but the coffin nails and screws and the shovels came from Pittsburg[h]. With hard woods and metals abounding, the corpse was hauled on a wagon from South Bend, Indiana. A hickory grove grew near by, but the pick and shovel handles came from New York. The cotton shirt on the dead man came from Cincinnati, the coat and breeches from Chicago, the shoes from Boston; the folded hands were encased in white gloves from New York, and round the poor neck, that had worn all its living days the bondage of lost opportunity, was twisted a cheap cravat from Philadelphia. That country, so rich in undeveloped resources, furnished nothing for the funeral except the corpse and the hole in the ground, and would probably have imported both of those if it could have done so. . . .

There are now more than $3,000,000 invested in marble quarries and machinery around that grave. Its pitiful loneliness is broken with the rumble of ponderous machines, and a strange tumult pervades the wilderness. Twenty miles away, the largest marble-cutting works in the world put to shame in a thousand shapes its modest headstone. Forty miles away four coffin factories, with their exquisite work, tempt the world to die. The iron hills are gashed and swarm with workmen. Forty cotton mills in a near radius weave infinite cloth that neighboring shops make into countless shirts. There are shoe factories, nail factories, shovel and pick factories, and carriage factories, to supply the other wants. And that country can now get up as nice a funeral, native and home-made, as you would wish to have.

The industrial growth of the South in the past ten years has been without precedent or parallel. It has been a great revolution, effected in peace. . . .

The race problem casts the only shadow that rests on the South. Truly the negro avenges the wrongs put upon him by the New England traders who brought him from Africa, and the Southern slave-holders who held him in bondage. . . .

Southern Beliefs Regarding Race Troubles.

First—That the whites shall have clear and unmistakable control of public affairs. They own the property. They have the intelligence. Theirs is the responsibility. For these reasons they are entitled to control. Beyond these reasons is a racial one. They are the superior race, and will not and cannot submit to the domination of an inferior race. . . .

Second—That the whites and blacks must walk in separate paths in the South. As near as may be, these paths should be made equal—but separate they must be now and always. This means separate schools, separate churches, separate accommodation everywhere—but equal accommodation where the same money is charged, or where the State provides for the citizen. Georgia gives her State University $8,000 a year; precisely the same sum to her colored university. . . .

Source: Henry W. Grady, *The New South* (New York: Robert Bonner's Sons, 1890), 188–91, 231, 239, 244–51.

The negroes of Georgia pay but one-fortieth of the taxes, and yet they take forty-nine per cent. of [*sic*] the school fund. Railroads in Georgia provide separate but equal cars for whites and blacks, and a white man is not permitted to occupy a colored car. This separation is not offensive to either race, but is accepted by both races as the best conducive to the common peace and prosperity. . . .

It must not be imagined that the negro is outlawed in the South. He has ten avenues of employment in this section to where he has one in the North. . . . Whatever the negro is fitted to do, he has abundant chance to do. All this, too, in the South, where the negro is in such numbers that he seriously competes for work and lowers wages. All this is done, too, without protest or without friction. . . .

On these two lines of action, political and social, the South has moved rapidly towards the solution of the race problem. If left alone, it can solve it. Interference simply irritates, and outside opinion simply misjudges. The negroes are prospering and are contented.

SOURCE 16.2 | *Testimony of North Carolina Industrial Workers* (1887)

How much of the New South ideal was rooted in reality? Southern industries still lagged behind their northern competitors. Southerners who took jobs in the region's new mills and mines found that industrial development did not necessarily lead to economic prosperity. In 1887 the North Carolina Bureau of Labor interviewed mill workers regarding their working conditions. The following excerpts offer insight into the lives of both employers and employees.

Durham

EMPLOYER: We have a very moral place; we have no drinking around our mill. In answering the question about the saving of earnings, we do not know just how many save their money, but we do know of several who have from $100 to $500 now, which they have saved up since they came to our place. Our operatives we think make as much and several of them more, than at any other mill in the State. They seem perfectly satisfied and we have had no trouble whatever in regard to strikes, etc. Our mill has only been running about two years and only a few have built houses, though several are speaking of it now.

EMPLOYEE: There are about 225 to 250 hands engaged at different classes of work in this mill, about 100 of them children—many of them very small children, under 12 years of age. Wages are about as good here as at any mill in the State and I think better than at many of them, the only trouble about wages is that

Source: W. N. Jones, *First Annual Report of the Bureau of Labor Statistics of the State of North Carolina* (1887), 149–50.

they are not paid in cash—trade checks are issued with which employees are expected to buy what they need at the company's store, which is not right. The same system is practised I am told, at most of the cotton mills in the State, but that does not make it right and just. The tobacco factories in this town pay the cash every week. Any man who has ever tried it knows there is a great difference in buying with the cash. This, with the long hours required for a day's work (12 hours), is the only cause for complaint: the officers are kind and close attention to work and sobriety and morality is required of all who work here. . . .

Randolph

EMPLOYEE: I work in the cotton mills. They employ men, women and children—many children who are too small to work, they should be at school; the parents are more to blame than are the mill-owners. The hands in the mills in this section are doing very well, and if they only received their pay weekly in cash instead of "trade checks," and store accounts, they would not complain if they were paid in cash and were allowed to buy for cash where they pleased, it would be much better. Ten hours are enough for a day's work. I believe the mills here would be willing to it if there was a law making all conform to it. I believe compulsory education would be a benefit too.

SOURCE 16.3 | *Sharecropper's Contract* (1882)

For all Henry Grady's pronouncements about the rise of industry, the majority of southern workers—white and black—continued to toil in the fields. Many found themselves forced to enter into sharecropping agreements with landlords like the Grimes family in Pitt County, North Carolina. This contract from the Grimes plantation reveals the extensive powers a landlord held over a sharecropper's labor.

To every one applying to rent land upon shares, the following conditions must be read and agreed to.

To every 30 or 35 acres, I agree to furnish the team, plow, and farming implements, except cotton planters, and I do not agree to furnish a cart to every cropper. The croppers are to have half of the cotton, corn, and fodder (and peas and pumpkins and potatoes if any are planted) if the following conditions are complied with, but—if not—they are to have only two-fifths. Croppers are to have no part or interest in the cotton seed raised from the crop planted and worked by them. No vine crops of any description, that is no watermelons . . . squashes or anything of that kind . . . are to be planted in the cotton or corn. All must work under my direction. All plantation work to be done by the croppers. . . .

Source: Grimes Family Papers (#3357), 1882. Southern Historical Collection, University of North Carolina, Chapel Hill.

All croppers must clean out stables and fill them with straw, and haul straw in front of stables whenever I direct. All the cotton must be manured, and enough fertilizer must be brought to manure each crop highly, the croppers to pay for one-half of all manure bought, the quantity to be purchased for each crop must be left to me.

No cropper is to work off the plantation when there is any work to be done on the land he has rented, or when his work is needed by me or other croppers. . . .

Every cropper must be responsible for all gear and farming implements placed in his hands, and if not returned must be paid for unless it is worn out by use.

Croppers must sow and plow in oats and haul them to the crib, but must have no part of them. Nothing to be sold from their crops, nor fodder, nor corn to be carried out of the fields until my rent is all paid, and all amounts they owe me and for which I am responsible are paid in full. . . .

The sale of every cropper's part of the cotton to be made by me when and where I choose to sell, and after deducting all they may owe me and all sums that I may be responsible for on their accounts, to pay them their half of the net proceeds. Work of every description, particularly the work on fences and ditches, to be done to my satisfaction, and must be done over until I am satisfied that it is done as it should be.

SOURCE 16.4 | *Mississippi Constitution* (1890)

By the end of the century, southern states had begun to codify the separation between whites and blacks—a thorny task considering that the Fourteenth and Fifteenth Amendments protected African Americans' civil and voting rights. The following excerpts from the Mississippi Constitution of 1890 show how southern officials rewrote the law to maintain white supremacy.

SEC. 207. Separate schools shall be maintained for children of the white and colored races. . . .

SEC. 243. A uniform poll tax of two dollars, to be used in aid of the common schools, and for no other purpose, is hereby imposed on every male inhabitant of this State between the ages of twenty-one and sixty years, except persons who are deaf and dumb or blind, or who are maimed by loss of hand or foot; said tax to be a lien only upon taxable property. The board of supervisors of any county may, for the purpose of aiding the common schools in that county, increase the poll tax in said county, but in no case shall the entire poll tax exceed in any one year three dollars on each poll. No criminal proceedings shall be allowed to enforce the collection of the poll tax.

SEC. 244. On and after the first day of January, A.D., 1892, every elector shall, in addition to the foregoing qualifications, be able to read any section of the

Source: Constitution of the State of Mississippi, Adopted November 1, 1890 (Jackson, MS: Clarion-Ledger, 1891), 47, 55, 61–62.

constitution of this State; or he shall be able to understand the same when read to him, or give a reasonable interpretation thereof. A new registration shall be made before the next ensuing election after January the first, A.D., 1892. . . .

SEC. 263. The marriage of a white person with a negro or mulatto, or person who shall have one-eighth or more of negro blood, shall be unlawful and void.

SEC. 264. No person shall be a grand or petit juror unless a qualified elector and able to read and write; but the want of any such qualification in any juror shall not vitiate any indictment or verdict. The legislature shall provide by law for procuring a list of persons so qualified, and the drawing therefrom of grand and petit jurors for each term of the circuit court.

SOURCE 16.5 | JUSTICE HENRY BILLINGS BROWN,
Plessy v. Ferguson (1896)

Homer Plessy was arrested after he refused to leave the whites-only section of a Louisiana railcar, even though he was actually seven-eighths white. Plessy hoped to build a test case around his arrest, and he sued the state of Louisiana, contending that its law separating whites and blacks on railroad cars violated the equal protection clause of the Fourteenth Amendment. In the decision in *Plessy v. Ferguson*, Justice Henry Billings Brown laid the underpinnings for the Jim Crow segregation that would dominate the South until the 1960s.

MR. JUSTICE BROWN, after stating the case, delivered the opinion of the court.

This case turns upon the constitutionality of an act of the General Assembly of the State of Louisiana, passed in 1890, providing for separate railway carriages for the white and colored races. . . . The constitutionality of this act is attacked upon the ground that it conflicts both with the Thirteenth Amendment of the Constitution, abolishing slavery, and the Fourteenth Amendment, which prohibits certain restrictive legislation on the part of the States.

1. That it does not conflict with the Thirteenth Amendment, which abolished slavery and involuntary servitude, except as a punishment for crime, is too clear for argument. Slavery implies involuntary servitude. . . .

    A statute which implies merely a legal distinction between the white and colored races—a distinction which is founded in the color of the two races and which must always exist so long as white men are distinguished from the other race by color—has no tendency to destroy the legal equality of the two races, or reestablish a state of involuntary servitude. Indeed, we do not understand that the Thirteenth Amendment is strenuously relied upon by the plaintiff in error in this connection.

2. By the Fourteenth Amendment, all persons born or naturalized in the United States and subject to the jurisdiction thereof are made citizens of the United

Source: *Plessy v. Ferguson*, 163 U.S. 537 (1896).

States and of the State wherein they reside, and the States are forbidden from making or enforcing any law which shall abridge the privileges or immunities of citizens of the United States, or shall deprive any person of life, liberty, or property without due process of law, or deny to any person within their jurisdiction the equal protection of the laws. . . .

The object of the amendment was undoubtedly to enforce the absolute equality of the two races before the law, but, in the nature of things, it could not have been intended to abolish distinctions based upon color, or to enforce social, as distinguished from political, equality, or a commingling of the two races upon terms unsatisfactory to either. Laws permitting, and even requiring, their separation in places where they are liable to be brought into contact do not necessarily imply the inferiority of either race to the other, and have been generally, if not universally, recognized as within the competency of the state legislatures in the exercise of their police power. The most common instance of this is connected with the establishment of separate schools for white and colored children, which has been held to be a valid exercise of the legislative power even by courts of States where the political rights of the colored race have been longest and most earnestly enforced. . . .

It is claimed by the plaintiff in error that, in any mixed community, the reputation of belonging to the dominant race, in this instance the white race, is property in the same sense that a right of action or of inheritance is property. Conceding this to be so for the purposes of this case, we are unable to see how this statute deprives him of, or in any way affects his right to, such property. If he be a white man and assigned to a colored coach, he may have his action for damages against the company for being deprived of his so-called property. Upon the other hand, if he be a colored man and be so assigned, he has been deprived of no property, since he is not lawfully entitled to the reputation of being a white man.

In this connection, it is also suggested by the learned counsel for the plaintiff in error that the same argument that will justify the state legislature in requiring railways to provide separate accommodations for the two races will also authorize them to require separate cars to be provided for people whose hair is of a certain color, or who are aliens, or who belong to certain nationalities, or to enact laws requiring colored people to walk upon one side of the street and white people upon the other, or requiring white men's houses to be painted white and colored men's black, or their vehicles or business signs to be of different colors, upon the theory that one side of the street is as good as the other, or that a house or vehicle of one color is as good as one of another color. The reply to all this is that every exercise of the police power must be reasonable, and extend only to such laws as are enacted in good faith for the promotion for the public good, and not for the annoyance or oppression of a particular class. . . .

Gauged by this standard, we cannot say that a law which authorizes or even requires the separation of the two races in public conveyances is unreasonable, or more obnoxious to the Fourteenth Amendment than the acts of Congress requiring separate schools for colored children in the District of Columbia, the constitutionality of which does not seem to have been questioned, or the corresponding acts of state legislatures.

We consider the underlying fallacy of the plaintiff's argument to consist in the assumption that the enforced separation of the two races stamps the colored race with a badge of inferiority. If this be so, it is not by reason of anything found in the act, but solely because the colored race chooses to put that construction upon it. The argument necessarily assumes that if, as has been more than once the case and is not unlikely to be so again, the colored race should become the dominant power in the state legislature, and should enact a law in precisely similar terms, it would thereby relegate the white race to an inferior position. We imagine that the white race, at least, would not acquiesce in this assumption. The argument also assumes that social prejudices may be overcome by legislation, and that equal rights cannot be secured to the negro except by an enforced commingling of the two races. We cannot accept this proposition. If the two races are to meet upon terms of social equality, it must be the result of natural affinities, a mutual appreciation of each other's merits, and a voluntary consent of individuals. . . . Legislation is powerless to eradicate racial instincts or to abolish distinctions based upon physical differences, and the attempt to do so can only result in accentuating the difficulties of the present situation.

INTERPRET THE EVIDENCE

1. According to Henry Grady, why was it important for the South to industrialize (Source 16.1)? How does Grady describe the relationship between whites and blacks in the South?

2. What was life like for southern mill workers (Source 16.2)? Do you think working in the mills provided any advantages over agricultural jobs? How did the employee at the Randolph cotton mill describe the working conditions?

3. What did the Grimes family provide for its sharecroppers (Source 16.3)? What did it expect in return? Why do you think anyone would enter into a sharecropping agreement?

4. How did the Mississippi Constitution of 1890 codify race and racial discrimination (Source 16.4)? Which statutes were explicitly based on race?

5. How does Justice Henry Billings Brown justify segregation (Source 16.5)? Whom does he blame if African Americans feel inferior because they are forced to sit in separate seating? Why does he believe that legislation cannot shape social change?

PUT IT IN CONTEXT

1. How "new" was the New South in terms of its labor conditions and its race relations?

PRIMARY SOURCE PROJECT **17**

The Meanings of Populism

▶ Compare the ideas that united the Populists with those that divided them.

During the final decade of the nineteenth century, farmers and workers organized politically in unprecedented ways. American laborers argued for a new kind of democracy, one more in line with their social and economic interests. Deciding that they would never meet their goals within the Republican or Democratic Parties, in 1892 farmers formed a third party, the People's Party, or the Populists (Source 17.4). Part of the success of the People's Party came from its expansive platform. Not only did it argue for the expansion of the monetary supply but it also called for federal ownership of communication and railroads, a government subtreasury to allow farmers to borrow money against the value of their stored crops, an eight-hour workday, and the right to vote for women. Many Populists argued that black and white farmers and workers should work together to force change (Source 17.2), and for a time the party managed to forge an interracial coalition.

People's Party candidates were elected to offices at the local and national level during the 1890s, and the party won electoral votes in the presidential election of 1892. But the party imploded following the defeat of William Jennings Bryan, the joint Populist-Democratic presidential candidate, four years later (Source 17.5). The Populist legacy, however, lived on into the twentieth century. Many of the social and political issues and policies of the Progressive and New Deal eras were rooted in the demands of the People's Party.

The following primary sources reveal the meanings of Populism for those who led and participated in the movement.

SOURCE 17.1 | FRANK DOSTER, *Labor Day Speech* (1894)

At the forefront of Populist politics and ideology was the relationship between the individual worker and the increasingly complex international economy. Frank Doster, who later served as chief justice of the Kansas Supreme Court, argued against monopolies in his remarks at a Labor Day rally in Topeka, Kansas, in 1894.

Everything which goes to sustain his physical life, which enables him to conduct his daily toil, which makes existence possible in this fierce competitive strife have become the monopoly of others—others to whom he sustains only the harshest and most exacting kind of contract relations. Formerly the tools of agriculture were the wagon and the plow; the tools of the worker in wood his plane and chisel and saw; the tools of the worker in iron his hammer and anvil and forge; and they were sufficient for all the purposes of industrial life. Now the terrible elements of physical nature which the gods can scarce bridle or control—steam, electricity, compressed air—are utilized to do the work of man. But these, the common property of all, have been made the monopoly of the few, have been turned aside from the beneficent ends for which designed, to serve the selfish purposes of avarice and greed. In the face of the power exerted by the monopolists of these tremendous engines of industry and commerce the republican and democratic parties stand paralyzed—hypnotized as it were, unable to control it or give it direction and shape for common good.

Against the tyrannical exercise of this power the People's Party in behalf of the laborers of the land protests. The failure to adapt the legislation of the country to the strange conditions which this new life has forced upon us is the cause in greater part of our industrial ills. . . .

The Populist Party proposes as the only means to the desired end to utilize the power of the combined whole, to bring the power of the social mass to bear upon the rebellious individuals who thus menace the peace and safety of the state. It says that the subjects of those monopolies and trusts are public in their nature, and that the powers exercised through them are in reality the functions and agencies of government itself. It would have the government, that is, the people, assert their rightful dominion over the same, and as the philosophic basis of its claim it prescribes at least two political formulae: One that it is the business of the government to do that for the individual which he cannot successfully do for himself, and which other individuals will not do for him upon just and equitable terms, the other, that the industrial system of a nation, like its political system, should be a government of and for and by the people alone.

Source: Norman Pollack, ed., *The Populist Mind* (Indianapolis: Bobbs-Merrill, 1967), 12–13.

SOURCE 17.2 | THOMAS E. WATSON, *The Negro Question in the South* (1892)

Not all Populists favored racial equality, but Tom Watson, the most prominent leader of the movement, called for incorporating African Americans into the Populist movement. In the following excerpt from the *Arena* magazine, Watson examines why, in his opinion, blacks would flee the Republican Party to join the Populists. In the early twentieth century, Watson became known for his demagoguery and anti-Semitism.

The key to the new political movement called the People's Party has been that the Democratic farmer was as ready to leave the Democratic ranks as the Republican farmer was to leave the Republican ranks. In exact proportion as the West received the assurance that the South was ready for a new party, it has moved. In exact proportion to the proof we could bring that the West had broken Republican ties, the South has moved. *Without* a decided break in both sections, neither would move. *With* that decided break, both moved.

The very same principle governs the race question in the South. The two races can never act together permanently, harmoniously, beneficially, till each race demonstrates to the other a readiness to leave old party affiliations and to form new ones, based upon the profound conviction that, in acting together, both races are seeking new laws which will benefit both. On no other basis under heaven can the "Negro Question" be solved.

Now, suppose that the colored man were educated upon these questions just as the whites have been; suppose he were shown that his poverty and distress came from the same sources as ours; suppose we should convince him that our platform principles assure him an escape from the ills he now suffers, and guarantee him the fair measure of prosperity his labor entitles him to receive,—would he not act just as the white Democrat who joined us did? Would he not abandon a party which ignores him as a farmer and laborer; which offers him no benefits of an equal and just financial system; which promises him no relief from oppressive taxation; which assures him of no legislation which will enable him to obtain a fair price for his produce?

Granting to him the same selfishness common to us all; granting him the intelligence to know what is best for him and the desire to attain it, why would he not act from that motive just as the white farmer has done?

That he would do so, is as certain as any future event can be made. Gratitude may fail; so may sympathy and friendship and generosity and patriotism; but in the long run, self-interest *always* controls. Let it once appear plainly that it is to the interest of a colored man to vote with the white man, and he will do it. Let it plainly appear that it is to the interest of the white man that the vote of the Negro should supplement his own, and the question of having that ballot freely cast and fairly counted, becomes vital to the *white man*. He will see that it is done.

Source: Thomas E. Watson, "The Negro Question in the South," *Arena* 4 (October 1892): 545–47, 550.

Now let us illustrate: Suppose two tenants on my farm; one of them white, the other black. They cultivate their crops under precisely the same conditions. Their labors, discouragements, burdens, grievances, are the same.

The white tenant is driven by cruel necessity to examine into the causes of his continued destitution. He reaches certain conclusions which are not complimentary to either of the old parties. He leaves the Democracy in angry disgust. He joins the People's Party. Why? Simply because its platform recognizes that he is badly treated and proposes to fight his battle. Necessity drives him from the old party, and hope leads him into the new. In plain English, he joins the organization whose declaration of principles is in accord with his conception of what he needs and justly deserves.

Now go back to the colored tenant. His surroundings being the same and his interests the same, why is it impossible for him to reach the same conclusions? Why is it unnatural for him to go into the new party at the same time and with the same motives?

Cannot these two men act together in peace when the ballot of the one is a vital benefit to the other? Will not political friendship be born of the necessity and the hope which is common to both? Will not race bitterness disappear before this common suffering and this mutual desire to escape it? Will not each of these citizens feel more kindly for the other when the vote of each defends the home of both? If the white man becomes convinced that the Democratic Party has played upon his prejudices, and has used his quiescence to the benefit of interests adverse to his own, will he not despise the leaders who seek to perpetuate the system? . . .

The question of social equality does not enter into the calculation at all. That is a thing each citizen decides for himself. No statute ever yet drew the latch of the humblest home—or ever will. Each citizen regulates his own visiting list—and always will.

The conclusion, then, seems to me to be this: the crushing burdens which now oppress both races in the South will cause each to make an effort to cast them off. They will see a similarity of cause and a similarity of remedy. They will recognize that each should help the other in the work of repealing bad laws and enacting good ones. They will become political allies, and neither can injure the other without weakening both. It will be to the interest of both that each should have justice. And on these broad lines of mutual interest, mutual forbearance, and mutual support the present will be made the stepping-stone to future peace and prosperity.

SOURCE 17.3 | *"Smith Wants Fair Division of Pie!"*
Political Cartoon (1900?)

The relationship between the Populists and African Americans was complex, but after 1896 the political connection between the two shattered. In this cartoon, Isaac Smith, a black Republican, chides C. H. Johnson, a Populist leader, for supporting a North Carolina election law that disfranchised blacks. Smith reminds Johnson that Populists had campaigned for African American votes in the past and accuses him of walking off without sharing any of the pie.

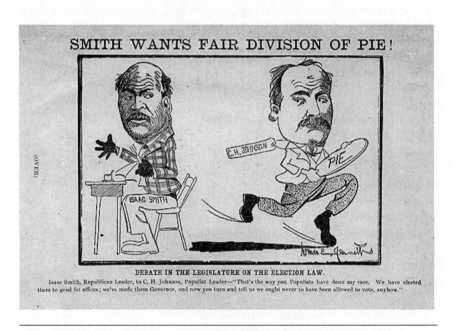

DEBATE IN THE LEGISLATURE ON THE ELECTION LAW.

Isaac Smith, Republican Leader, to C. H. Johnson, Populist Leader—"That's the way you Populists have done my race. We have elected them to good fat offices; we've made them Governor, and now you turn and tell us we ought never to have been allowed to vote, anyhow."

Documenting the American South, University Library, The University of North Carolina Library at Chapel Hill

SOURCE 17.4 | *The People's Party Tree* (1895)

Populist newspapers and periodicals published hundreds of political cartoons illustrating the party's proposals. This cartoon, which appeared in the Cherryville *Kansas Populist* in 1895, relates Populist demands to the history of American political parties.

Daily Kansas Populist (Cherryvale) August 23, 1895

SOURCE 17.5 | WILLIAM JENNINGS BRYAN, *Cross of Gold Speech* (1896)

William Jennings Bryan of Nebraska stormed onto the political scene in 1896. The Democrats nominated him to challenge incumbent William McKinley for president, and, seeing that Bryan favored some of the same policies, in particular the free and unlimited coinage of silver, the People's Party backed him and nominated Tom Watson for vice president. But Bryan could not defeat the Republican coalition of corporate forces and urban workers, and the Populists collapsed after the election. Bryan ran unsuccessfully for president three more times. His 1896 Cross of Gold speech earned him the Democratic nomination and established him as a compelling orator.

Never before in the history of this country has there been witnessed such a contest as that through which we have passed. Never before in the history of American politics has a great issue been fought out, as this issue has been, by the voters themselves.

On the 4th of March, 1895, a few Democrats, most of them members of Congress, issued an address to the Democrats of the nation asserting that the money question was the paramount issue of the hour; asserting also the right of a majority of the Democratic Party to control the position of the party on this paramount issue; concluding with the request that all believers in free coinage of silver in the Democratic Party should organize and take charge of and control the policy of the Democratic Party. Three months later, at Memphis, an organization was perfected, and the silver Democrats went forth openly and boldly and courageously proclaiming their belief and declaring that if successful they would crystallize in a platform the declaration which they had made; and then began the conflict with a zeal approaching the zeal which inspired the crusaders who followed Peter the Hermit. Our silver Democrats went forth from victory unto victory, until they are assembled now, not to discuss, not to debate, but to enter up the judgment rendered by the plain people of this country.

But in this contest, brother has been arrayed against brother, and father against son. The warmest ties of love and acquaintance and association have been disregarded. Old leaders have been cast aside when they refused to give expression to the sentiments of those whom they would lead, and new leaders have sprung up to give direction to this cause of freedom. Thus has the contest been waged, and we have assembled here under as binding and solemn instructions as were ever fastened upon the representatives of a people.

We do not come as individuals. . . . I say it was not a question of persons; it was a question of principle; and it is not with gladness, my friends, that we find ourselves brought into conflict with those who are now arrayed on the other side. . . .

When you come before us and tell us that we shall disturb your business interests, we reply that you have disturbed our business interests by your action.

Source: *Official Proceedings of the Democratic National Convention Held in Chicago, Illinois, July 7, 8, 9, 10, and 11, 1896* (Logansport, IN, 1896), 227–29, 231, 233–34.

We say to you that you have made too limited in its application the definition of a businessman. The man who is employed for wages is as much a businessman as his employer. The attorney in a country town is as much a businessman as the corporation counsel in a great metropolis. The merchant at the crossroads store is as much a businessman as the merchant of New York. The farmer who goes forth in the morning and toils all day, begins in the spring and toils all summer, and by the application of brain and muscle to the natural resources of this country creates wealth, is as much a businessman as the man who goes upon the Board of Trade and bets upon the price of grain. The miners who go a thousand feet into the earth or climb 2,000 feet upon the cliffs and bring forth from their hiding places the precious metals to be poured in the channels of trade are as much businessmen as the few financial magnates who in a backroom corner the money of the world.

We come to speak for this broader class of businessmen. . . .

Now, my friends, let me come to the great paramount issue. If they ask us here why it is we say more on the money question than we say upon the tariff question, I reply that if protection has slain its thousands the gold standard has slain its tens of thousands. If they ask us why we did not embody all these things in our platform which we believe, we reply to them that when we have restored the money of the Constitution, all other necessary reforms will be possible, and that until that is done there is no reform that can be accomplished. . . .

There are two ideas of government. There are those who believe that if you just legislate to make the well-to-do prosperous, that their prosperity will leak through on those below. The Democratic idea has been that if you legislate to make the masses prosperous, their prosperity will find its way up and through every class that rests upon it.

You come to us and tell us that the great cities are in favor of the gold standard. I tell you that the great cities rest upon these broad and fertile prairies. Burn down your cities and leave our farms, and your cities will spring up again as if by magic. But destroy our farms and the grass will grow in the streets of every city in the country. . . .

It is the issue of 1776 over again. Our ancestors, when but 3 million, had the courage to declare their political independence of every other nation upon earth. Shall we, their descendants, when we have grown to 70 million, declare that we are less independent than our forefathers? No, my friends, it will never be the judgment of this people. Therefore, we care not upon what lines the battle is fought. If they say bimetallism is good but we cannot have it till some nation helps us, we reply that, instead of having a gold standard because England has, we shall restore bimetallism, and then let England have bimetallism because the United States have.

If they dare to come out in and in the open defend the gold standard as a good thing, we shall fight them to the uttermost, having behind us the producing masses of the nation and the world. Having behind us the commercial interests and the laboring interests and all the toiling masses, we shall answer their demands for a gold standard by saying to them, you shall not press down upon the brow of labor this crown of thorns. You shall not crucify mankind upon a cross of gold.

INTERPRET THE EVIDENCE

1. According to Frank Doster, how had the position of the worker deteriorated at the end of the nineteenth century (Source 17.1)? How did the People's Party work to change this system?

2. Compare Thomas E. Watson's views on Populists and African Americans (Source 17.2) with those expressed by Isaac Smith (Source 17.3).

3. How does the "People's Party Tree" cartoon express the relationship between the People's Party and the two major parties (Source 17.4)? Why do you think the Populists relied so heavily on cartoons such as this one and Source 17.3?

4. What is William Jennings Bryan's argument in his Cross of Gold speech (Source 17.5)? According to Bryan, why is money the primary political issue? How does he appeal to history in his speech? What political drawbacks were there in relying on the money issue above the rest of the Populist platform?

PUT IT IN CONTEXT

1. What do you think made the Populist message appealing? How did the Populists differ from the two major parties? Why do you think their third-party effort failed?

Class and Leisure in the American City

> ▶ Explain how gender, class, ethnicity, and the urban environment shaped the writers or the subjects of these primary sources.

Few historical events altered the American landscape like the rise of the city at the turn of the twentieth century. Population demographics changed as increasing numbers of immigrants, primarily from southern and eastern Europe, poured into urban areas. These immigrants brought their own traditions and customs, increasing the diversity of city life (Source 18.3). Urban dwellers also participated in new forms of leisure and consumerism. Amusement parks like New York City's Coney Island, nickelodeons, dance halls, and sporting events such as boxing matches became national pastimes (Sources 18.1 and 18.2).

The new cities accentuated class differences at the same time that they offered ways for people of different classes to share social spaces. The working classes flocked to take part in new, inexpensive forms of urban leisure. Wealthier people sought to distance themselves from the working people they often saw at Coney Island and other city attractions (Source 18.5). Instead, they attended symphony concerts and the opera and socialized in exclusive clubs. This world of urban amusements also disrupted traditional gender roles. Many working-class women took advantage of the anonymity of the city to ignore gender norms and express their independence (Source 18.4). Some reformers gasped at areas where men and women could congregate freely.

The following primary sources illuminate the social and cultural changes that occurred in the twentieth-century city.

SOURCE 18.1 | *Elephant Ride at Coney Island* (1911)

By 1900 Coney Island had been transformed from a sleepy New York resort town into a busy center of commercialized leisure. Its beaches and parks drew both working- and middle-class audiences for adventure and thrills or just for an escape from the city. In this photo, visitors enjoy several different attractions, including watching women take a ride on an elephant.

Library of Congress, LC-B2-2207-13

SOURCE 18.2 | *International Contest for the Heavyweight Championship* (1907)

Boxing also emerged as a popular pastime during this period. Although some reformers were outraged by the sport's violence, prizefighting drew large crowds in cities across the country. The following still shows action from a July 4, 1907, heavyweight championship fight between Tommy Burns and Bill Squires in Ocean View, California.

SOURCE 18.3 | JOSEPH RUMSHINSKY, *The Living Orphan* (1914)

As immigrants streamed into the cities of the Northeast, they brought their cultural traditions, including music, with them. Joseph Rumshinsky arrived in the United States from his native Vilna, Lithuania, in 1904. He rapidly became one of the most prominent Jewish composers in America. The following song, translated from Yiddish, is an example of a more genteel strain of immigrant song craft.

O living orphan
You uprooted tree.
You have no home, no rest
Since your mother's not there.
There's no one to take care of you
And tenderly put you to sleep
And pray to God for your help:
Mama, Mama, where are you now?

Source: Mark Slobin, *Tenement Songs: The Popular Music of Jewish Immigrants* (Urbana: University of Illinois Press, 1982), 127.

SOURCE 18.4 | HUTCHINS HAPGOOD, *Types from City Streets* (1910)

In 1910 journalist, author, and cultural observer Hutchins Hapgood published *Types from City Streets*, which he described as "a volume of sketches intended to throw light upon the charm of what from one point of view is the 'ordinary' person—careless, human, open, democratic." In the following excerpt, he describes the social lives of shop girls in New York City's Bowery section.

The "Spieler" Girl of the Bowery

The dance-hall is truly a passion with working-girls. The desire to waltz is bred in the feminine bone. It is a familiar thing to see little girls on the East Side dancing rhythmically on the street, to the music of some hand-organ, while heavy wagons roll by unheeded. When those little girls grow older and become shop-girls they often continue to indulge their passion for the waltz. Some of them dance every night, and are so confirmed in it that they are technically known as "spielers." Many a girl, nice girl, too, loves the art so much that she will dance with any man she meets, whatever his character or appearance. Often two girls will go to

Source: Hutchins Hapgood, *Types from City Streets* (New York: Funk and Wagnalls, 1910), 134–37.

some dance-hall, which may or may not be entirely respectable, and deliberately look for men to dance with. On one occasion, at a Harlem dancing-place, where all kinds of working-girls go, I saw a girl compel her escort, a man who could not dance, to ask men she had never met, and whom he did not know, to dance with her. A girl of that character may never want to see her fellow waltzer again, but many of these girls get involved with undesirable men, simply through their uncontrollable passion for the waltz. When carried to an excess, it is as bad as drink or gambling.

Girls of the "spieler" class of society are of an extreme simplicity, too simple even to be practical. They lack the hardness of the swell department-store girls; but make up for it by their "toughness"; which . . . is the conventional atmosphere of the Bowery. They strive to be nothing but what they are, and altho they, as a rule, express little, what they do express is characteristic. They have no false refinement; no refinement, indeed, in the acquired sense, but they have that kind of distinction which results from a simplicity of feeling and experience due to their lives being near "de limit."

I met one of these little Bowery "spieler" girls, who, too independent to stay at home, spent $2.50 a week for food and room and the other $2.50 of her $5.00 salary for clothes and amusements. She could get what she deemed a good meal for fifteen cents, but ordinarily spent only five or ten cents. Her mind was as simple as her life; she had no ideas, but everything she said was as real as poverty and as significant as the sounds made by the instinctive animals.

I went one day, with this little girl and a relative of hers — an ex-pickpocket — to a wedding-reception in one of the lower wards of the city, where I had an opportunity to see what "the people" are like. Imagine a little room about twelve by eight feet, crowded with truck-drivers and hod-carriers [brick carriers] and factory girls and tailor-girls — as many as fifteen or twenty — all lined up against the wall drinking beer, except a few who were dancing wildly in the middle of the room, stepping indiscriminately upon the toes of the others and spilling beer in great quantities over the floor. Altho the orgy had begun three days before, and the third cask of beer had been broached, yet the sternest moralist would have found nothing wrong with the occasion. It was "low," to be sure, and exceedingly free, but nobody did anything he was ashamed of. The bride danced with everybody and kissed almost everybody; and almost everything was said. Nothing could exceed the affair for freedom. But the utmost un-selfconsciousness prevailed. The only person who was at all aware of himself was the ex-thief. He was the swellest person in the room, and looked uncomfortable when his shoes were inundated with beer. He was also the only person who seemed unfortunate or unhappy. Surely, Walt Whitman would have reveled in the scene: for here were human beings as lacking in misery and respectability as even the great poet could desire.

SOURCE 18.5 | THORSTEIN VEBLEN, *The Theory of the Leisure Class* (1899)

In his landmark 1899 book, *The Theory of the Leisure Class*, economist Thorstein Veblen argued that the wealthier classes looked for ways to distinguish themselves from the poor as working-class urban dwellers sought new leisure and amusement pursuits. In the following excerpts, Veblen discusses his ideas of "conspicuous leisure" and "conspicuous consumption."

Abstention from labour is not only a honorific or meritorious act, but it presently comes to be a requisite of decency. The insistence on property as the basis of reputability is very naïve and very imperious during the early stages of the accumulation of wealth. Abstention from labour is the conventional evidence of wealth and is therefore the conventional mark of social standing; and this insistence on the meritoriousness of wealth leads to a more strenuous insistence on leisure. . . .

But the whole of the life of the gentleman of leisure is not spent before the eyes of the spectators who are to be impressed with that spectacle of honorific leisure which in the ideal scheme makes up his life. For some part of the time his life is perforce withdrawn from the public eye, and of this portion which is spent in private the gentleman of leisure should, for the sake of his good name, be able to give a convincing account. He should find some means of putting in evidence the leisure that is not spent in the sight of the spectators. This can be done only indirectly, through the exhibition of some tangible, lasting results of the leisure so spent—in a manner analogous to the familiar exhibition of tangible, lasting products of the labour performed for the gentleman of leisure by handicraftsmen and servants in his employ. . . .

The quasi-peaceable gentleman of leisure, then, not only consumes of the staff of life beyond the minimum required for subsistence and physical efficiency, but his consumption also undergoes a specialisation as regards the quality of the goods consumed. He consumes freely and of the best, in food, drink, narcotics, shelter, services, ornaments, apparel, weapons and accoutrements, amusements, amulets, and idols or divinities. In the process of gradual amelioration which takes place in the articles of his consumption, the motive principle and the proximate aim of innovation is no doubt the higher efficiency of the improved and more elaborate products for personal comfort and well-being. But that does not remain the sole purpose of their consumption. The canon of reputability is at hand and seizes upon such innovations as are, according to its standard, fit to survive. Since the consumption of these more excellent goods is an evidence of wealth, it becomes honorific; and conversely, the failure to consume in due quantity and quality becomes a mark of inferiority and demerit.

This growth of punctilious discrimination as to qualitative excellence in eating, drinking, etc., presently affects not only the manner of life, but also the training and intellectual activity of the gentleman of leisure. He is no longer simply

---

Source: Thorstein Veblen, *The Theory of the Leisure Class: An Economic Study of Institutions* (London: Macmillan, 1912), 41, 43–44, 73–75.

the successful, aggressive male, the man of strength, resource, and intrepidity. In order to avoid stultification he must also cultivate his tastes, for it now becomes incumbent on him to discriminate with some nicety between the noble and the ignoble in consumable goods. He becomes a connoisseur, in creditable viands [provisions] of various degrees of merit, in manly beverages and trinkets, in seemly apparel and architecture, in weapons, games, dancers, and the narcotics. This cultivation of the aesthetic faculty requires time and application, and the demands made upon the gentleman in this direction therefore tend to change his life of leisure into a more or less arduous application to the business of learning how to live a life of ostensible leisure in a becoming way. . . .

Conspicuous consumption of valuable goods is a means of reputability to the gentleman of leisure.

INTERPRET THE EVIDENCE

1. What are the various amusements you can see in the photo of Coney Island (Source 18.1)? What can you tell about the audiences Coney Island is hoping to attract with these rides? Why would riding an elephant be interesting to early twentieth-century Americans?

2. What kind of crowd attended the heavyweight boxing fight (Source 18.2)? How is it different from the Coney Island crowd? How does the still portray the fight? What does the audience reveal about the popularity of boxing?

3. What is the subject of Joseph Rumshinsky's song "The Living Orphan" (Source 18.3)? How would you describe Rumshinsky's lyrical approach?

4. How does Hutchins Hapgood describe the nightlife of East Side shop girls (Source 18.4)? What role did dancing play in these women's lives? Why might stories like this have been controversial?

5. According to Thorstein Veblen, what is the value of leisure and consumption for the wealthy (Source 18.5)? Do you think he is critical of consumerism? Why or why not?

PUT IT IN CONTEXT

1. How did urban leisure, commerce, and entertainment differ depending on a person's gender, economic class, and ethnicity?

2. How did urbanization make changes in consumerism and leisure possible?

Progressivism and Social Control

▶ Analyze the assumptions behind the moral and social reforms the progressives supported.

At its core, progressivism was a response to the unsettling forces of rapid industrialization, corporate capitalism, urbanization, and immigration. Although the Populists of the 1890s addressed similar grievances, they focused more on the economic plight of rural Americans than did progressives. Progressivism emerged a decade later during relative prosperity and tended to originate in cities of the East and Midwest. Progressives shared common concerns as consumers, urban residents, and political citizens. In their search for political, economic, social, and cultural order, they supported a variety of reforms, including direct primary elections, conservation measures, the abolition of child labor, and the regulation of trusts, banks, and railroads.

Often forgotten in the history of these reforms is the extent to which progressives sought to control the behavior of people they considered morally deficient and a danger to civilization. Unlike governmental reforms that aimed to expand democracy and political participation, progressives' efforts to impose their moral values on the rest of the population ignored the wishes of ordinary people. Progressives favored policies that reflected their own brand of middle-class morality and targeted the behavior of immigrants, the working classes, women of questionable character, and nonwhites. What these progressives called moral reform—prohibition (Source 19.1), antivice campaigns (Source 19.2), immigration restriction (Source 19.4)—poor and working-class families often saw as an invasion of their privacy and a threat to their way of life (Source 19.5). The eugenics movement, which sought to maintain white racial purity through selective breeding, represented the most sinister form of progressive reform (Source 19.3). While some eugenicists advocated birth control for the poor, others favored sterilization for those deemed "undesirable." By 1931 more than thirty states had passed laws allowing the forced sterilization of people with mental or physical disabilities, as well as individuals from socially disadvantaged groups.

SOURCE 19.1 | FRANCES WILLARD, *On Behalf of Home Protection* (1884)

Frances Willard was an educator and a dean of the Women's College of Northwestern University. She became president of the Woman's Christian Temperance Union (WCTU) in 1879 and served in that position until her death in 1898. Willard wrote a history of the WCTU that included reflections on how she became an advocate for both prohibition and women's suffrage at an early age.

Longer ago than I shall tell, my father returned one night to the far-off Wisconsin home where I was reared; and, sitting by my mother's chair, with a child's attentive ear, I listened to their words. He told us of the news that day [that] had brought about Neal Dow [mayor of Portland, Maine, who sponsored Maine's prohibition law] and the great fight for prohibition down in Maine, and then he said: "I wonder if poor, rum-cursed Wisconsin will ever get a law like that?" And mother rocked a while in silence in the dear old chair I love, and then she gently said: "Yes, Josiah, there'll be such a law all over the land some day, when women vote."

My father had never heard her say so much before. He was a great conservative; so he looked tremendously astonished, and replied, in his keen, sarcastic voice: "And pray how will you arrange it so that women shall vote?" Mother's chair went to and fro a little faster for a minute, and then, not looking into his face, but into the flickering flames of the grate, she slowly answered: "Well, I say to you, as the apostle Paul said to his jailor, 'You have put us into prison, we being Romans, and you must come and take us out.' "

That was a seed-thought in a girl's brain and heart. Years passed on, in which nothing more was said upon this dangerous theme. My brother grew to manhood, and soon after he was twenty-one years old he went with his father to vote. Standing by the window, a girl of sixteen years, a girl of simple, homely fancies, not at all strong-minded, and altogether ignorant of the world, I looked out as they drove away, my father and my brother, and as I looked I felt a strange ache in my heart, and tears sprang to my eyes. Turning to my sister Mary, who stood beside me, I saw that the dear little innocent seemed wonderfully sober, too. I said: "Don't you wish we could go with them when we are old enough? Don't we love our country just as well as they do?" and her little frightened voice piped out: "Yes, of course we ought. Don't I know that? but you mustn't tell a soul—not mother, even; we should be called strong-minded."

In all the years since then I have kept these things, and many others like them, and pondered them in my heart; but two years of struggle in this temperance reform have shown me, as they have ten thousand other women, so clearly and so impressively, my duty, that I have passed the Rubicon [a limiting boundary] of silence, and am ready for any battle that shall be involved in this honest declaration of faith that is within me. . . .

Source: Frances Willard, *Women and Temperance; or, The Work and Workers of the Woman's Christian Temperance Union* (Hartford, CT: Park Publishing, 1884), 457–59.

I thought that women ought to have the ballot as I paid the hard-earned taxes upon my mother's cottage home—but I never said as much—somehow the motive did not command my heart. For my own sake, I had not the courage, but I have for thy sake, dear native land, for thy necessity is as much greater than mine as thy transcendent hope is greater than the personal interest of thy humble child. . . .

Ah, it is women who have given the costliest hostages to fortune. Out into the battle of life they have sent their best beloved, with fearful odds against them, with snares that men have legalized and set for them on every hand. Beyond the arms that held them long, their boys have gone forever. Oh! by the danger they have dared; by the hours of patient watching over beds where helpless children lay; by the incense of ten thousand prayers wafted from their gentle lips to Heaven, I charge you give them power to protect, along life's treacherous highway, those whom they have so loved. Let it no longer be that they must sit back among the shadows, hopelessly mourning over their strong staff broken, and their beautiful rod; but when the sons they love shall go forth to life's battle, still let their mothers walk beside them, sweet and serious, and clad in the garments of power.

SOURCE 19.2 | *Abstinence Poster* (1919)

This poster is one of forty-eight produced by the U.S. Public Health Service for its "Keeping Fit" campaign, a sex education program aimed at adolescent boys that stressed moral and physical fitness. Here a fast-talking "wise guy" tries to persuade an innocent-looking youth to overlook the possibly serious consequences of sexual promiscuity.

University of Minnesota Libraries, Social Welfare History Archives

SOURCE 19.3 | *Indiana Sterilization Law* (1907)

Many progressives embraced eugenics—a pseudoscience that advocated selective breeding to improve the quality of human beings—as a way to combat social ills that they thought derived from hereditary factors. The popularity of eugenics among progressives at the turn of the twentieth century led to the passage of measures like Indiana's Compulsory Sterilization Law of 1907, which promoted forced sterilization to prevent people with mental and physical defects or other "undesirable" traits from procreating.

Whereas, Heredity plays a most important part in the transmission of crime, idiocy, and imbecility;

Penal Institutions—Surgical Operations.

Therefore, *Be it enacted by the general assembly of the State of Indiana,* That on and after the passage of this act it shall be compulsory for each and every institution in the state, entrusted with the care of confirmed criminals, idiots, rapists, and imbeciles, to appoint upon its staff, in addition to the regular institutional physician, two skilled surgeons of recognized ability, whose duty it shall be, in conjunction with the chief physician of the institution, to examine the mental and physical condition of such inmates as are recommended by the institutional physician and board of managers. If, in the judgment of this committee of experts and the board of managers, procreation is inadvisable and there is no probability of improvement of the mental condition of the inmate, it shall be lawful for the surgeons to perform such operation for the prevention of procreation as shall be decided safest and most effective. But this operation shall not be performed except in cases that have been pronounced unimprovable: *Provided,* That in no case shall the consultation fee be more than three dollars to each expert, to be paid out of the funds appropriated for the maintenance of such institution.

Source: *Acts 1907, Laws of the State of Indiana, Passed at the Sixty-fifth Regular Session of the General Assembly* (Indianapolis: William B. Burford, 1907), 377–78.

SOURCE 19.4 | *The Immigration Act of 1917*

The wave of immigrants arriving from eastern and southern Europe between 1890 and 1914 prompted strenuous efforts to restrict immigration. Labor unions worried that an oversupply of cheap labor would drive down wages. Native-born whites, whose Protestant ancestors had arrived generations earlier, feared that the newer, primarily Jewish and Catholic immigrants endangered their moral and cultural values. In 1917 Congress enacted legislation to reduce the influx of foreigners. The new law included the following provisions outlining who should be denied entry.

Source: Immigration Act of 1917, 39 Stat. 875–76 (1917).

Sec. 3. That the following classes of aliens shall be excluded from admission into the United States: All idiots, imbeciles, feeble-minded persons, epileptics, insane persons; persons who have had one or more attacks of insanity at any time previously; persons of constitutional psychopathic inferiority; persons with chronic alcoholism; paupers; professional beggars; vagrants; persons afflicted with tuberculosis in any form or with a loathsome or dangerous contagious disease; persons not comprehended within any of the foregoing excluded classes who are found to be and are certified by the examining surgeon as being mentally or physically defective, such physical defect being of a nature which may affect the ability of such alien to earn a living; persons who have been convicted of or admit having committed a felony or other crime or misdemeanor involving moral turpitude; polygamists, or persons who practice polygamy or believe in or advocate the practice of polygamy; anarchists, or persons who believe in or advocate the overthrow by force or violence of the Government of the United States, or of all forms of law, or who disbelieve in or are opposed to organized government, or who advocate the assassination of public officials, or who advocate or teach the unlawful destruction of property; persons who are members of or affiliated with any organization entertaining and teaching disbelief in or opposition to organized government, or who advocate or teach the duty, necessity, or propriety of the unlawful assaulting or killing of any officer or officers, either of specific individuals or of officers generally, of the Government of the United States or of any other organized government, because of his or their official character, or who advocate or teach the unlawful destruction of property; prostitutes, or persons coming into the United States for the purpose of prostitution or for any other immoral purpose; persons who directly or indirectly procure or attempt to procure or import prostitutes or persons for the purpose of prostitution or for any other immoral purpose; persons who are supported by or receive in whole or in part the proceeds of prostitution; persons hereinafter called contract laborers, who have been induced, assisted, encouraged, or solicited to migrate to this country by offers or promises of employment, whether such offers or promises are true or false, or in consequence of agreements, oral, written or printed, express or implied, to perform labor in this country of any kind, skilled or unskilled; persons who have come in consequence of advertisements for laborers printed, published, or distributed in a foreign country; persons likely to become a public charge; persons who have been deported under any of the provisions of this Act, and who may again seek admission within one year from the date of such deportation, unless prior to their reembarkation at a foreign port or their attempt to be admitted from foreign contiguous territory the Secretary of Labor shall have consented to their reapplying for admission; persons whose tickets or passage is paid for with the money of another, or who are assisted by others to come, unless it is affirmatively and satisfactorily shown that such persons do not belong to one of the foregoing excluded classes; persons whose ticket or passage is paid for by any corporation, association, society, municipality, or foreign Government, either directly or indirectly; stowaways, except that any such stowaway, if otherwise admissible, may be admitted in the discretion of the Secretary of Labor; all children under sixteen years of age, unaccompanied by or not coming to one or both of their parents, except that any such children may, in the discretion of the Secretary of Labor, be admitted if in his opinion they are not likely to become a public charge and are otherwise eligible.

SOURCE 19.5 | *Sanitary Precaution* (c. 1914)

Although progressives' interest in public health and sanitation was generally motivated by a sincere desire to prevent the spread of disease, these concerns were often closely linked to racial and ethnic anxieties. Immigration opponents, for example, argued that certain immigrant groups, by virtue of an inherent disposition toward uncleanliness, posed a direct threat to public health. The cartoon here suggests a similar link between African American servants and the spread of disease.

INTERPRET THE EVIDENCE

1. What role does Frances Willard suggest women should play in controlling the behavior of men (Source 19.1)? What light does Willard's memoir shed on the role of motherhood in shaping progressive values?

2. What connection does the abstinence poster make between disease and vice (Source 19.2)? What do you make of the absence of a direct moral argument against promiscuity in the poster?

3. Why was eugenics so attractive to many progressive reformers (Source 19.3)?

4. Who benefited and who lost from immigration restriction laws (Source 19.4), temperance laws, and antiprostitution laws?

5. What racial assumptions lie behind the cartoon on health threats (Source 19.5)?

PUT IT IN CONTEXT

1. How did the progressives' emphasis on disease reflect their larger vision of American society at the turn of the twentieth century?

2. How did progressives' understanding of the sources of disease shape the kinds of "cures" they proposed for America's ills?

The Committee on Public Information and Wartime Propaganda

▶ Evaluate the various persuasive strategies and rhetorical assumptions used to mobilize support for the war effort.

Woodrow Wilson won reelection in 1916 under the campaign slogan, "He kept us out of the war." However, by the next year he realized that American involvement would be crucial. He recognized that bringing the United States into the war would be unpopular and sought ways to convince Americans to support U.S. involvement in World War I in Europe. By establishing the Committee on Public Information (CPI) under the leadership of journalist George Creel in 1917, shortly after the United States entered the war, Wilson hoped to launch a propaganda campaign that could capture the hearts and minds of unsure Americans. Creel embraced the cause. "We fought prejudice, indifference, and disaffection at home," he wrote in 1920, "and we fought ignorance and falsehood abroad." In fighting this battle "for the verdict of mankind," Creel's CPI favored emotional appeals over nuanced analysis. It used patriotic lecturers, created cartoons that demonized the Germans, targeted appeals toward laborers and teachers (Source 20.3), and published pamphlets that encouraged women to do their part in the war effort. The government even commissioned films to increase American morale. "There was no medium of appeal that we did not employ," Creel recalled.

The CPI's mobilization was impressive. Creel boasted that his largest corps of speakers, the Four-Minute Men, delivered over 750,000 speeches during the war (Source 20.1). The CPI compiled more than 1,400 drawings to support U.S. involvement in the war (Sources 20.2 and 20.4). The following documents provide examples of this government effort to gain support for American involvement in World War I, as well as Creel's answer to critics who characterized the CPI as a censorship committee (Source 20.5).

SOURCE 20.1 | POEM READ BY FOUR-MINUTE MEN, *It's Duty Boy* (c. 1918)

One of the CPI's popular programs was the Four-Minute Men, a group of 75,000 volunteers, men and women, who delivered speeches at movie theaters, concerts, parades, labor halls, and other public venues. Their speeches were carefully written by the CPI to encourage public support on topics ranging from food conservation to enlistment. Below is one of the poems read by Four-Minute Men.

My boy must never bring disgrace to his immortal sires—
At Valley Forge and Lexington they kindled freedom's fires,
John's father died at Gettysburg, mine fell at Chancellorsville;
While John himself was with the boys who charged up San Juan Hill.
And John, if he was living now, would surely say with me,
"No son of ours shall e'er disgrace our grand old family tree
By turning out a slacker when his country needs his aid."
It is not of such timber that America was made.
I'd rather you had died at birth or not been born at all,
Than know that I had raised a son who cannot hear the call
That freedom has sent round the world, its previous rights to save—
This call is meant for you, my boy, and I would have you brave;
And though my heart is breaking, boy, I bid you do your part,
And show the world no son of mine is cursed with craven heart;
And if, perchance, you ne'er return, my later days to cheer,
And I have only memories of my brave boy, so dear,
I'd rather have it so, my boy, and know you bravely died
Than have a living coward sit supinely by my side.
To save the world from sin, my boy, God gave his only son—
He's asking for My boy, to-day, and may His will be done.

Source: Reprinted in Alfred Cornebise, *War As Advertised: The Four Minute Men and America's Crusade, 1917–1918* (Philadelphia: American Philosophical Society, 1984), http://historymatters .gmu.edu/d/4970.

SOURCE 20.2 | *Halt the Hun!* (c. 1918)

The most iconic legacy of the Committee on Public Information is the hundreds of cartoons the agency published. Often accompanied by dramatic text, these vivid images appealed to viewers' emotions. The following cartoon warns of the potential consequences if Americans fail to purchase war bonds.

Library of Congress, LC-USZC4-2792

SOURCE 20.3 | *Advertisement in* History Teacher's Magazine (1917)

Pamphlets, broadsides, and advertisements in popular magazines all made the case for why the United States should enter the war and for how American civilians could bolster the war effort at home. The following advertisement appeared in *History Teacher's Magazine* in September 1917.

The Committee on Public Information
Established by Order of the President, April 4, 1917

Distribute free *except as noted* the following publications :

I. Red, White and Blue Series :

No. 1. How the War Came to America (English, German, Polish, Bohemian, Italian, Spanish and Swedish).

No. 2. National Service Handbook (primarily for libraries, schools, Y. M. C. A.'s, Clubs, fraternal organizations, etc., as a guide and reference work on all forms of war activity, civil, charitable and military).

No. 3. The Battle Line of Democracy. Prose and Poetry of the Great War. Price 25 cent. Special price to teachers. Proceeds to the Red Cross. Other issues in preparation.

II. War Information Series :

No. 1. The War Message and Facts Behind it.

No. 2. The Nation in Arms, by Secretaries Lane and Baker.

No. 3. The Government of Germany, by Prof. Charles D. Hazen.

No. 4. The Great War from Spectator to Participant.

No. 5. A War of Self Defense, by Secretary Lansing and Assistant Secretary of Labor Louis F. Post.

No. 6. American Loyalty by Citizens of German Descent.

No. 7. Amerikanische Bürgertreue, a translation of No. 6.

Other issues will appear shortly.

III. Official Bulletin :

Accurate daily statement of what all agencies of government are doing in war times. Sent free to newspapers and postmasters (to be put on bulletin boards). Subscription price $5.00 per year.

Address Requests to

Committee on Public Information, Washington, D. C.

What Can History Teachers Do Now?

You can help the community realize what history should mean to it.

You can confute those who by selecting a few historic facts seek to establish some simple cure-all for humanity.

You can confute those who urge that mankind can wipe the past off the slate and lay new foundations for civilization.

You can encourage the sane use of experience in discussions of public questions.

You can help people understand what democracy is by pointing out the common principle in the ideas of Plato, Cromwell, Rousseau, Jefferson, Jackson and Washington.

You can help people understand what German autocracy has in common with the autocracy of the Grand Mogul.

You can help people understand that democracy is not inconsistent with law and efficient government.

You can help people understand that failure of the past to make the world safe for democracy does not mean that it can not be made safe in the future.

You can so teach your students that they will acquire "historical mindedness" and realize the connection of the past with the present.

You can not do these things unless you inform your self, and think over your information.

You can help yourself by reading the following:

"History and the Great War" bulletin of Bureau of Education.

A series of articles published throughout the year in THE HISTORY TEACHER'S MAGAZINE.

You can obtain aid and advice by writing to

The National Board for Historical Service, 1133 Woodward Building, Washington, D. C.

United States Bureau of Education, Division of Civic Education, Washington, D. C.

Committee on Public Information, Division of Educational Co-operation, 10 Jackson Place, Washington, D. C.

The Committee on Patriotism through Education of the National Security League, 31 Pine Street, New York City.

Carnegie Endowment for International Peace, 2 Jackson Place, Washington, D. C.

National Committee of Patriotic and Defense Societies, Southern Building, Washington, D. C.

The World Peace Foundation, 40 Mount Vernon St., Boston, Mass.

American Association for International Conciliation, 407 West 117th Street, New York City.

The American Society for Judicial Settlement of International Disputes, Baltimore, Md.

The Editor, THE HISTORY TEACHER'S MAGAZINE, Philadelphia.

SOURCE 20.4 | *He Will Come Back a Better Man!* (1918)

CPI materials argued that intervention in World War I would benefit the nation in numerous ways, including having a positive effect on the young men who wore the uniform in combat. The following advertisement, which first appeared in the *Outlook* magazine, details how a soldier would "come back a better man" after the war.

SOURCE 20.5 | GEORGE CREEL, *The "Censorship" Bugbear* (1920)

As head of the CPI, George Creel publicly defended its work against criticism. Opponents focused on censorship, charging that the CPI threatened the freedom of the press. In this excerpt from his 1920 book, *How We Advertised America*, Creel discusses censorship and his belief that the CPI did not violate Americans' rights and liberties.

The initial disadvantages and persistent misunderstandings that did so much to cloud public estimation of the Committee had their origin in the almost instant antagonism of the metropolitan press. At the time of my appointment a censorship bill was before Congress, and the newspapers, choosing to ignore the broad sweep of the Committee's functions, proceeded upon the exclusive assumption that I was to be "the censor." As a result of press attack and Senate discussion, the idea became general and fixed that the Committee was a machinery of secrecy and repression organized solely to crush free speech and a free press.

As a matter of fact, I was strongly opposed to the censorship bill, and delayed acceptance of office until the President had considered approvingly the written statement of my views on the subject. It was not that I denied the need of some sort of censorship, but deep in my heart was the feeling that the desired results could be obtained without paying the price that a formal law would have demanded. Aside from the physical difficulties of enforcement, the enormous cost, and the overwhelming irritation involved, I had the conviction that our hope must lie in the aroused patriotism of the newspaper men of America.

With the nation in arms, the need was not so much to keep the press from doing the hurtful things as to get it to do the helpful things. It was not servants we wanted, but associates. Better far to have the desired compulsions proceed from within than to apply them from without. Also, for the first time in our history, soldiers of the United States were sailing to fight in a foreign land, leaving families three thousand miles behind them. Nothing was more important than that there should be the least possible impairment of the people's confidence in the printed information presented to them. Suspicious enough by reason of natural anxieties, a censorship law would have turned every waiting heart over to the fear that news was being either strangled or minimized.

Aside from these considerations, there was the freedom of the press to bear in mind. No other right guaranteed by democracy has been more abused, but even these abuses are preferable to the deadening evil of autocratic control. In addition, it is the inevitable tendency of such legislation to operate solely against the weak and the powerless, and, as I pointed out, the European experience was thick with instances of failure to proceed against great dailies for bold infraction. . . .

My proposition, in lieu of the proposed law, was a voluntary agreement that would make every paper in the land its own censor, putting it up to the patriotism and common sense of the individual editor to protect purely military information of tangible value to the enemy.

Source: George Creel, *How We Advertised America* (New York: Harper and Brothers Publishers, 1920), 16–18.

INTERPRET THE EVIDENCE

1. In the poem "It's Duty Boy," in what ways is World War I compared to previous American wars (Source 20.1)? What does the poem imply about the reasons America is involved in World War I? How does the poem use positive and negative emotions to encourage young men to enlist in the military?

2. How does the "Halt the Hun!" cartoon portray the German soldiers (Source 20.2)? How does the cartoon appeal to Americans' sense of pride? To gender norms?

3. Why would the CPI target history teachers (Source 20.3)? What did the advertisement encourage teachers to do in their classrooms?

4. According to the CPI, how would men benefit from war service (Source 20.4)? Who is the audience for this advertisement? What does it suggest were the proper roles for women during wartime?

5. Why did George Creel oppose a federal censorship law (Source 20.5)? Do you think Creel's alternative plan left the door open for censorship?

PUT IT IN CONTEXT

1. Do you think the federal government has the responsibility to marshal popular support for war efforts? Why or why not? What are the potential positive and negative effects of such government action?

The Scopes "Monkey Trial"

▶ Explain the political, cultural, and regional differences that shaped the different viewpoints about faith, science, and the Scopes trial.

In the culture clashes of the 1920s, one of the most prominent battlegrounds was evolution. Modernists accepted Darwin's theories as valid scientific principle, while traditionalists believed evolution a blasphemous challenge to the Genesis creation story (Sources 21.4 and 21.5). More broadly, religious fundamentalists felt the era's urban intellectualism would destroy the rural, Protestant America they loved. When Tennessee banned the teaching of evolution (Source 21.1), the American Civil Liberties Union (ACLU) advertised for someone to test this law. Local business leaders in the eastern Tennessee town of Dayton persuaded high school science teacher John Scopes to do so, hoping a trial would generate publicity. Neither they nor Scopes was prepared for the firestorm that followed. Both sides saw this case as a struggle for the soul of America, and journalists from around the country flocked to Dayton. It was the first trial in U.S. history to be broadcast live on radio.

Adding to the growing media circus were the attorneys who volunteered for each side. Leading Scopes's team was Clarence Darrow, a colorful and famous defense attorney who sat on the ACLU's national committee (Source 21.2). Representing the prosecution was William Jennings Bryan, a three-time Democratic presidential candidate whose politics were long synonymous with rural values and fundamentalism (Source 21.3).

Was America a modern cosmopolitan society or one based on rural Protestantism? The outcome of the case satisfied neither side. Scopes was found guilty and given a $100 fine, but fundamentalism suffered widespread ridicule. When Bryan himself took the stand as an expert witness, Darrow's persistent questioning led Bryan to assert a literal interpretation of the Bible and then defend it by stating he believed, for example, that the world was created in six days. The press mercilessly mocked Bryan, turning him into a symbol of religious bigotry and ignorance.

The documents that follow offer a number of different viewpoints about faith, science, and the trial.

SOURCE 21.1 | *The Butler Act* (1925)

The Butler Act, as it became known, was introduced by John Washington Butler, a farmer and member of the Tennessee House of Representatives. Butler was a fan of William Jennings Bryan and shared his concern that science was undermining a belief in traditional religious values. The legislation would be upheld by the Tennessee Supreme Court in 1927 and remained law until its repeal in 1967.

House Bill No. 185

Butler

An Act prohibiting the teaching of the Evolution Theory in all the Universities, Normals and all other public schools of Tennessee, which are supported in whole or in part by the public school funds of the State, and to provide penalties for the violations thereof.

SECTION 1. BE IT ENACTED BY THE GENERAL ASSEMBLY OF THE STATE OF TENNESSEE, That it shall be unlawful for any teacher in any of the Universities, normal and all other public schools of the State which are supported in whole or in part by the public school funds of the state, to teach any theory that denies the story of the Divine Creation of man as taught in the Bible, and to teach instead that man has descended from a lower order of animals.

SECTION 2. BE IT FURTHER ENACTED, That any teacher found guilty of the violation of this Act, shall be guilty of a misdemeanor and upon conviction, shall be fined not less than One Hundred ($100.00) Dollars nor more than Five Hundred ($500.00) Dollars for each offense.

SECTION 3. BE IT FURTHER ENACTED, That this Act take effect from and after its passage the public welfare requiring it. Passed March 13, 1925.

W. F. Barry
Speaker of the House of Representatives

L. D. Hill
Speaker of the Senate

Approved: Austin Peay
Governor
March 21st, 1925

Source: "Butler Act," National Science Education Center, http://ncse.com/files/pub/legal /Scopes/Butler_Act.pdf.

SOURCE 21.2 | CLARENCE DARROW, *Trial Speech* (July 13, 1925)

When he volunteered for the Scopes trial, Clarence Darrow was already known as a brilliant and controversial defense attorney. He built a national reputation defending labor radicals and accused murderers and fighting the death penalty. The following excerpt, from one of Darrow's speeches before the court on the second day of the trial, displays his characteristic wit in analyzing the legal consequences of the Butler Act.

Let's see now. Can your Honor tell what is given as the origin of man as shown in the Bible? Is there any human being who can tell us? There are two conflicting accounts in the first two chapters. There are scattered all through it various acts and ideas, but to pass that up for the sake of argument, no teacher in any school in the state of Tennessee can know that he is violating a law, but must test every one of its doctrines by the Bible, must he not? . . .

[The law] does not specify what you cannot teach, but says you cannot teach anything that conflicts with the Bible. Then just imagine making a criminal code that is so uncertain and impossible that every man must be sure that he has read everything in the Bible and not only read it but understands it, or he might violate the criminal code. Who is the chief mogul that can tell us what the Bible means? He or they should write a book and make it plain and distinct, so we would know. Let us look at it. There are in America at least 500 different sects or churches, all of which quarrel with each other over the importance and nonimportance of certain things or the construction of certain passages. All along the line they do not agree among themselves and cannot agree among themselves. They never have and probably never will. There is a great division between the Catholics and the Protestants. There is such a disagreement that my client, who is a schoolteacher, not only must know the subject he is teaching, but he must know everything about the Bible in reference to evolution. And he must be sure that he expresses his right or else some fellow will come along here, more ignorant perhaps than he and say, "You made a bad guess and I think you have committed a crime." No criminal statute can rest that way.

Source: Clarence Darrow, Speech in Defense of Religious Liberty, in *The World's Most Famous Court Trial: Tennessee Evolution Case* (1925; reprint, Dayton, TN: Rhea County Historical Society, 1978).

SOURCE 21.3 | WILLIAM JENNINGS BRYAN, *Trial Speech* (July 16, 1925)

Throughout William Jennings Bryan's long political career, his fame rested on his oratorical skills and his championing of rural America. Both of these characteristics were on display in Tennessee. The following selection is from one of Bryan's many long speeches during the trial. In it, he focuses on the religious and political rights of Tennesseans and also pokes fun at the evolutionary link between humans and monkeys.

No, not the Bible, you see in this state they cannot teach the Bible.[1] They can only teach things that declare it to be a lie, according to the learned counsel. These people in the state—Christian people—have tied their hands by their Constitution. They say we all believe in the Bible for it is the overwhelming belief in the state, but we will not teach that Bible which we believe even to our children through teachers that we pay with our money. No, no, it isn't the teaching of the Bible, and we are not asking it. The question is can a minority in this state come in and compel a teacher to teach that the Bible is not true and make the parents of these children pay the expenses of the teacher to tell their children what these people believe is false and dangerous? Has it come to a time when the minority can take charge of a state like Tennessee and compel the majority to pay their teachers while they take religion out of the heart of the children of the parents who pay the teachers?

. . .

So, my friends, if that were true, if man and monkey were in the same class, called primates, it would mean they did not come up from the same order. It might mean that instead of one being the ancestor of the other they were all cousins. But it does not mean that they did not come from the lower animals, if this is the only place they could come from, and the Christian believes man came from above, but the evolutionist believes he must have come from below.

Source: William Jennings Bryan, First Speech, in *The World's Most Famous Court Trial: Tennessee Evolution Case* (1925; reprint, Dayton, TN: Rhea County Historical Society, 1978).

[1]Bryan exaggerated slightly. Tennessee law had for the previous decade provided for daily Bible readings in the public schools.

SOURCE 21.4 | *Cartoon from the* Chicago Defender (June 20, 1925)

Many anti-evolutionists liked to critique Darwin's claim that humankind descended from apes. In the following cartoon, the *Chicago Defender*, a prominent African American newspaper, pokes fun at this argument. Although the Scopes trial was not about white supremacy, the *Defender* took this opportunity to comment on both evolution and southern racism.

Used with the permission of the *Chicago Defender*

SOURCE 21.5 | *Poem by Mrs. E. P. Blair,* Nashville Tennessean (June 29, 1925)

While men such as William Jennings Bryan were the national faces of anti-evolutionism, it was women who made up a majority of the movement's rank-and-file membership. The following poem is a window into the thoughts and passions of one of these female activists.

Between Truth and Error, Right and Wrong,
    The fight is on.
For country, God and mother's song,
    It must be won!
Go sound the alarm, go gather your forces,
    Oh Tennessee!
Land of the pioneer, home of the volunteer,
    The daring, the free

The hearthstone, the college, the temple, and even
    Our God's great throne,
The star-crowned heroes, both the quick and the dead
    Are calling their own.
You heard the call down all the ages
    When might found right.
With your hands, your blood, and your life
    You've won the fight.

Now Error, the monster, calls forth her cohorts
    From sea to sea,
They come from earth's four corners down
    To Tennessee.
They challenge your power to rule your own
    Your rights deny.
They scoff at you, ridicule you,
    Your laws defy.

Their forces are clad in garments great,
    Of science and law.
With the camouflage cloak of knowledge
    To hide their claw
Go look at the havoc and heartache of nations
    Where they passed through.
Their blasting breath has meant instant death
    To the noble and true.

Source: Mrs. E. P. Blair, "The Battle Hymn of Tennessee," *Nashville Tennessean,* June 29, 1925, 2.

God made this His battleground, for you've
    Been wise and true.
Earth's unborn, its children, mothers and nations
    Are calling to you.
So Tennessee, light your candle of wisdom!
    Your altar of prayer!
And the God of Truth fire and inspire you,
    To do and to dare!

INTERPRET THE EVIDENCE

1. What does the Butler Act (Source 21.1) reveal about religious objections to Darwin's theory of evolution? How does it interpret the role of the government in the educational system?

2. How does Clarence Darrow (Source 21.2) make his case on legal grounds? In what ways is he defending religious liberty? Why does he think the Butler Act is dangerous?

3. In what ways is William Jennings Bryan (Source 21.3) making an argument for states' rights? Why would he make an appeal for the rights of majorities? How does he try to challenge evolution?

4. How does the *Chicago Defender* cartoon (Source 21.4) connect the debate over evolution to southern racial practices? Why does the cartoonist include the U.S. Capitol in the background?

5. What does Mrs. Blair's poem (Source 21.5) reveal about anti-evolutionists' view of gender roles in the 1920s? On what grounds, and on whose behalf, does she defend the Butler Act?

PUT IT IN CONTEXT

1. Why was the scientific idea of evolution a threat to rural America in the 1920s?

2. Explain how the Scopes trial was a debate about the role of education in American society.

Franklin Roosevelt's New Deal and Its Critics

▶ Evaluate the ways in which Roosevelt and his opponents attempted to make their viewpoints acceptable to a larger audience.

Franklin Roosevelt won four presidential elections between 1932 and 1944. His Democratic coalition outlived him and dominated American politics for decades. Many New Deal programs, such as Social Security, remain the under-pinning of the American welfare state. Despite these apparent successes, the New Deal met constant opposition. Even as many destitute Americans welcomed Roosevelt's programs, the New Deal proved a political flash point. The president endorsed an unprecedented expansion of federal power, and he recognized early on that he had to persuade reluctant Americans that government programs would benefit them (Sources 22.1 and 22.2).

Some people were not convinced. The Republican Party led the opposition (Source 22.4), but criticism of the New Deal also proved bipartisan. The southern wing of the Democratic coalition believed in states' rights and sometimes bristled at the president's sweeping federal programs (Source 22.3). The Supreme Court ruled key New Deal legislation unconstitutional. Some critics, such as Huey P. Long (Source 22.5), believed that Roosevelt was not doing enough to solve the nation's problems.

As the following documents reveal, debates over the New Deal dominated American politics in the years between Roosevelt's election and the beginning of World War II.

SOURCE 22.1 | FRANKLIN ROOSEVELT, Fireside Chat
Transcript (May 7, 1933)

Shortly after taking office, Franklin Roosevelt took to the airwaves to explain his New Deal to the American public. Fireside chats allowed Roosevelt to address large numbers of Americans by radio as they sat in their homes, making his words feel more personal. The following transcript contains excerpts of Roosevelt's May 7, 1933 fireside chat, an address also filmed and shown in theaters. The newly elected president outlined his plans and discussed many of the themes that would characterize the New Deal through the rest of the decade.

00:00:00

PRESIDENT FRANKLIN D. ROOSEVELT:—which is about to pass legislation that will briefly ease the mortgage distress among the farmers and among the home-owners of the nation, by providing for the easing of the burden of debt that now bears so heavily upon millions of our people.

00:00:24

Well considered and conservative measures will likewise be proposed within a few days, that will attempt to give to the industrial workers of the country a more fair wage return, to prevent cutthroat competition, to prevent unduly long hours for labor, and at the same time, to encourage each industry to prevent overproduction.

00:00:50

I have no expectation of making a hit every time I—to bat. What I seek is the high-est possible batting average, not only for myself, but for the team. Theodore Roosevelt once said to me, "If I can be right 75 percent of the time, I shall come up to the fullest measure of my hopes."

00:01:13

To the people of this country, all of us in Washington, the members of the Congress and the members of this administration, owe a profound debt of gratitude. Throughout the Depression, you have been patient. You have granted us wide powers. You have encouraged us with a widespread approval of our purposes. Every ounce of strength, every resource at our command, we have devoted and we are devoting to the end of justifying your confidence.

00:01:48

We are encouraged to believe that a wise and sensible beginning has been made. In the present spirit of mutual confidence and the present spirit of mutual encouragement, we go forward.

SOURCE 22.2 | Give a Man a Job! *Transcript* (1933)

Roosevelt's numerous allies included the burgeoning Hollywood film industry. The following transcript is from a film produced by the Hollywood studio Metro-Goldwyn-Mayer and starring the actor Jimmy Durante. The clip used humor and song to express support for Roosevelt and to propose ways in which American employers could contribute to economic recovery.

00:00:00

[orchestral music]
[audience applauding]

00:00:25

JIMMY DURANTE: [singing to music] You and you and you and you, you've got a
   President now. He gave the land a New Deal. You hold the cards, now you
   deal. You and you and you and you and you put shoulders to the plough. He
   gave us what we asked fer, now pay him back somehow. Step out in front, get
   back of the President, and give a man a job. He bore the brunt, now bear with
   the President, and give a man a job. If the old name of Roosevelt makes the
   old heart throb, you take this message straight from the President and give a
   man a job.

00:01:11

You look like a banker. Who drives your car?
MALE AUDIENCE MEMBER 1: I drive it myself, but have a cigar.
JIMMY DURANTE: Keep your cigar and hire a chauffeur and keep a man from
   becoming a loafer.
You look like a grocer.
MALE AUDIENCE MEMBER 2: No, sir. My job's extermination.

00:01:26

JIMMY DURANTE: You must give your assistants each a nice weekend vacation.
MALE AUDIENCE MEMBER 2: And I'll need more men to kill the rats.
JIMMY DURANTE: We want you to hire a crowd. You do good work if you hang out
   this sign. [handing him a National Recovery Administration (NRA) poster] It
   means "No Rats Allowed."
What's the matter with you?
FEMALE AUDIENCE MEMBER: I'm a very sick woman.
JIMMY DURANTE: Oh, a hypo-crondiac. You'd best get a doctor for pneumonia, a
   doctor for insomnia, one for osmosis, and two for halitosis.

00:01:56

One for amenia and one for exczemia, neuritis, bronchitis, phlebitis, St. Vitus or
   any other kind of an -itis, that will delight us. You must get a doctor for every
   disease you've got, and that way he'll give you lots of enjoyment. And in that
   way, Madam, you will help to end unemployment.
Now listen to me, everybody. Step up in front, get back of him, get back of the
   President, and give a man a job.
You know he bore the brunt, you know that, I know it. So step up and give a man
   a job. You know who's in back of this signia of NRA? No? Well, I'll tell you.
   And when I do, it'll give your heart a trump.

00:02:36

You take this message straight from the President and give—a—man—a job. [cheering and applause]

SOURCE 22.3 | *Packing the Supreme Court: Two Views, Political Cartoons* (1937)

In his first term, President Roosevelt secured legislation to implement his New Deal; however, by 1937 the Supreme Court had overturned several key pieces of New Deal legislation, arguing that Congress had exceeded its constitutional authority. As the Social Security Act and the National Labor Relations Act came up for review before the Court, Roosevelt tried to dilute the influence of the Court's conservative majority. Following his landslide reelection in 1936, he asked Congress to enlarge the Court so that he could appoint justices more favorable to his liberal agenda.

THE GREAT EMANCIPATOR—1937

Franklin D. Roosevelt Library

To Six of the Nine

The Granger Collection, New York

SOURCE 22.4 | *Republican Party National Platform* (1936)

The Republican Party opposed many of the programs of the Democratic Roosevelt, and it hoped to retake the presidency in 1936. It endorsed a platform highly critical of the New Deal and its results (or lack thereof). In the 1936 election, Roosevelt and his vice president, John Nance Garner, won a landslide victory over Republican presidential candidate Alfred M. Landon and his running mate, Colonel Frank Knox.

America is in peril. The welfare of American men and women and the future of our youth are at stake. We dedicate ourselves to the preservation of their political liberty, their individual opportunity and their character as free citizens, which today for the first time are threatened by Government itself.

Source: Donald Bruce Johnson, comp., *National Party Platforms*, rev. ed., 2 vols. (Urbana: University of Illinois Press, 1978), 1:360.

For three long years the New Deal Administration has dishonored American traditions and flagrantly betrayed the pledges upon which the Democratic Party sought and received public support.

The powers of Congress have been usurped by the President.

The integrity and authority of the Supreme Court have been flouted.

The rights and liberties of American citizens have been violated.

Regulated monopoly has displaced free enterprise.

The New Deal Administration constantly seeks to usurp the rights reserved to the States and to the people.

It has insisted on the passage of laws contrary to the Constitution.

It has intimidated witnesses and interfered with the right of petition.

It has dishonored our country by repudiating its most sacred obligations.

It has been guilty of frightful waste and extravagance, using public funds for partisan political purposes.

It has promoted investigations to harass and intimidate American citizens, at the same time denying investigations into its own improper expenditures.

It has created a vast multitude of new offices, filled them with its favorites, set up a centralized bureaucracy, and sent out swarms of inspectors to harass our people.

It has bred fear and hesitation in commerce and industry, thus discouraging new enterprises, preventing employment and prolonging the depression.

It secretly has made tariff agreements with our foreign competitors, flooding our markets with foreign commodities.

It has coerced and intimidated voters by withholding relief to those opposing its tyrannical policies.

It has destroyed the morale of our people and made them dependent upon government.

Appeals to passion and class prejudice have replaced reason and tolerance.

To a free people, these actions are insufferable. This campaign cannot be waged on the traditional differences between the Republican and Democratic parties. The responsibility of this election transcends all previous political divisions. We invite all Americans, irrespective of party, to join us in defense of American institutions.

SOURCE 22.5 | HUEY P. LONG, *Criticism of Franklin Roosevelt* (1935)

Roosevelt also faced opposition from the political left. Before his assassination in 1935, Huey Pierce Long of Louisiana stood poised to challenge Roosevelt. In the following speech, delivered on the radio March 7, 1935, and entered into the *Congressional Record* five days later, Long describes what he saw as the limitations of the New Deal and the flaws of the president.

Source: *Congressional Record*, March 12, 1935.

The kitchen cabinet that sat in to advise Hoover was not different from the kitchen cabinet which advised Roosevelt. . . .

Why, do you think this Roosevelt's plan for plowing up cotton, corn, and wheat; and for pouring milk in the river, and for destroying and burying hogs and cattle by the millions, all while people starve and go naked—do you think those plans were the original ideas of this Roosevelt administration? If you do, you are wrong. The whole idea of that kind of thing first came from Hoover's administration. . . .

Now, my friends, when this condition of distress and suffering among so many millions of our people began to develop in the Hoover administration, we knew then what the trouble was and what we would have to do to correct it. . . .

I said then, as I have said since, that it was inhuman to have food rotting, cotton and wool going to waste, houses empty, and at the same time to have millions of our people starving, naked, and homeless because they could not buy the things which other men had and for which they had no use whatever. So we convinced Mr. Franklin Delano Roosevelt that it was necessary that he announce and promise to the American people that in the event he were elected President of the United States he would pull down the size of the big man's fortune and guarantee something to every family—enough to do away with all poverty and to give employment to those who were able to work and education to the children born into the world. Mr. Roosevelt made those promises; he made them before he was nominated in the Chicago convention. He made them again before he was elected in November, and he went so far as to remake those promises after he was inaugurated President of the United States. And I thought for a day or two after he took the oath as President, that maybe he was going through with his promises. No heart was ever so saddened; no person's ambition was ever so blighted, as was mine when I came to the realization that the President of the United States was not going to undertake what he had said he would do, and what I know to be necessary if the people of America were ever saved from calamity and misery.

So now, my friends, I come to that point where I must in a few sentences describe to you just what was the cause of our trouble which became so serious in 1929, and which has been worse ever since. The wealth in the United States was three times as much in 1910 as it was in 1890, and yet the masses of our people owned less in 1910 than they did in 1890. . . .

But what did we do to correct that condition? Instead of moving to take these big fortunes from the top and spreading them among the suffering people at the bottom, the financial masters of America moved in to take complete charge of the Government for fear our lawmakers might do something along that line. And as a result, 14 years after the report of 1916, the Federal Trade Commission made a study to see how the wealth of this land was distributed, and did they find it still as bad as it was in 1916? They found it worse! They found that 1 percent of the people owned about 59 percent of the wealth, which was almost twice as bad as what was said to be an intolerable condition in 1916, when 2 percent of the people owned 60 percent of the wealth. . . .

Remember, in 1916 there was a middle class—33 percent of the people—who owned 35 percent of the wealth. That middle class is practically gone today. It no longer exists. They have dropped into the ranks of the poor.

INTERPRET THE EVIDENCE

1. In his May 1933 fireside chat, what does Franklin Roosevelt highlight as the important concepts that will guide the New Deal (Source 22.1)? How would you characterize the tone of his address?

2. According to the "Give a Man a Job!" transcript, how could Americans best take advantage of Roosevelt's programs (Source 22.2)? What was the relationship between business and patriotism?

3. Analyze how the two political cartoons (Source 22.3) on Roosevelt's attempt to change the membership of the Supreme Court use images and symbols to persuade different audiences.

4. According to the Republican Party platform of 1936, how had the Roosevelt administration and the New Deal harmed the country (Source 22.4)?

5. According to Huey P. Long, why had the New Deal failed (Source 22.5)? What did he argue that Roosevelt should do to alleviate poverty?

PUT IT IN CONTEXT

1. How did supporters and opponents of the New Deal differ in their vision of the role of government in the economy?

2. How much did the New Deal change political and economic conditions in the United States?

Anti-Japanese Prejudice during World War II

▶ Analyze the arguments for placing Japanese Americans, including those who were citizens, into internment camps and evaluate the response of the internees to their situation.

As it had during World War I, the United States government marshaled its resources to increase public support for involvement in World War II (Source 23.1). Videos, posters, and pamphlets all declared the worthiness of the cause and the moral necessity of going to fight. Also as in World War I, these appeals often used stereotypes to depict the enemy, and the Japanese faced unprecedented discrimination during the war (Source 23.2). The U.S. government portrayed the Japanese homeland in a negative light, and under Executive Order 9066, signed by President Franklin D. Roosevelt, it forced Japanese Americans, many of them U.S. citizens, out of their homes and businesses and into internment camps. They received no help from the Supreme Court, which upheld the validity of the order (Sources 23.3 and 23.4).

The following documents offer insight into the experience of Japanese Americans in World War II. Government propaganda portrayed the Japanese in a way designed to elicit an emotional response from Americans of European descent. A majority of Supreme Court justices agreed that the Japanese were a risk to society. Yet the Japanese internees persisted as best they could, and many filed lawsuits and agitated politically for fair treatment. Although imprisoned in camps, they maintained their dignity and demonstrated many forms of creativity (Source 23.5).

SOURCE 23.1 | *Monica Sone Remembers Pearl Harbor* (1953)

Few Americans would forget where they were or how they felt when they first learned of the Japanese attack on Pearl Harbor. The following document describes the experience of Monica

Source: Monica Sone, *Nisei Daughter* (Boston: Little, Brown, 1953), 145–46.

Sone, an American-born woman (*Nisei*) of Japanese immigrant parents (*Isei*). At the time of the Japanese attack on Pearl Harbor on December 7, 1941, Sone was a student at the University of Washington. Sone and her family were eventually placed in an internment camp in Idaho.

On a peaceful Sunday morning, December 7, 1941, Henry, Sumi, and I were at choir rehearsal singing ourselves hoarse in preparation for the annual Christmas recital of Handel's "Messiah." Suddenly Chuck Mizuno, a young University of Washington student, burst into the chapel, gasping as if he had sprinted all the way up the stairs.

"Listen, everybody!" he shouted. "Japan just bombed Pearl Harbor . . . in Hawaii. It's war!"

The terrible words hit like a blockbuster, paralyzing us. Then we smiled feebly at each other, hoping this was one of Chuck's practical jokes. Miss Hara, our music director, rapped her baton impatiently on the music stand and chided him, "Now Chuck, fun's fun, but we have work to do. Please take your place. You're already half an hour late."

But Chuck strode vehemently back to the door. "I mean it, folks, honest! I just heard the news over my car radio. Reporters are talking a blue streak. Come on down and hear it for yourselves."

. . . I felt as if a fist had smashed my pleasant little existence, breaking it into jigsaw puzzle pieces. An old wound opened up again, and I found myself shrinking inwardly from my Japanese blood, the blood of an enemy. I knew instinctively that the fact that I was an American by birthright was not going to help me escape the consequences of this unhappy war.

One girl mumbled over and over again, "It can't be, God, it can't be!" Someone else was saying, "What a spot to be in! Do you think we'll be considered Japanese or Americans?"

A boy replied quietly, "We'll be Japs, same as always. But our parents are enemy aliens now, you know."

A shocked silence followed.

SOURCE 23.2 | *Poster to All Persons of Japanese Ancestry* (1942)

Following Executive Order 9066, federal officials implemented a plan to remove people of Japanese descent from the West Coast. The following text comes from a poster that was displayed in San Francisco, California. It reveals the government's strategy and the sacrifices that Japanese residents had to make.

Western Defense Command and Fourth Army Wartime Civil Control Administration

Presidio of San Francisco, California

Source: U.S. Army, Western Defense Command, *Final Report: Japanese Evacuation from the West Coast, 1942* (Washington, D.C.: Government Printing Office, 1943), 99–100.

May 3, 1942

Instructions to All Persons of Japanese Ancestry Living in the Following Area:

All of that portion of the County of Alameda, State of California, within the boundary beginning at the point where the southerly limits of the City of Oakland meet San Francisco Bay; thence easterly and following the southerly limits of said city to U.S. Highway No. 50; thence southerly and easterly on said Highway No. 50 to its intersection with California State Highway No. 21; thence southerly on said Highway No. 21 to its intersection, at or near Warm Springs, with California State Highway No. 17; thence southerly on said Highway No. 17 to the Alameda-Santa Clara County line; thence westerly and following said county line to San Francisco Bay; thence northerly, and following the shoreline of San Francisco Bay to the point of beginning.

Pursuant to the provisions of Civilian Exclusion Order No. 34, this Headquarters, dated May 3, 1942, all persons of Japanese ancestry, both alien and non-alien, will be evacuated from the above area by 12 o'clock noon, P.W.T., Saturday, May 9, 1942.

No Japanese person living in the above area will be permitted to change residence after 12 o'clock noon, P.W.T., Sunday, May 3, 1942, without obtaining special permission from the representative of the Commanding General, Northern California Sector, at the Civil Control Station located at:

920 "C" Street,
Hayward, California.

Such permits will only be granted for the purpose of uniting members of a family, or in cases of grave emergency.

The Civil Control Station is equipped to assist the Japanese population affected by this evacuation in the following ways:

1. Give advice and instructions on the evacuation.

2. Provide services with respect to the management, leasing, sale, storage or other disposition of most kinds of property, such as real estate, business and professional equipment, household goods, boats, automobiles and livestock.

3. Provide temporary residence elsewhere for all Japanese in family groups.

4. Transport persons and a limited amount of clothing and equipment to their new residence.

The Following Instructions Must Be Observed:

1. A responsible member of each family, preferably the head of the family, or the person in whose name most of the property is held, and each individual living alone, will report to the Civil Control Station to receive further instructions.

This must be done between 8:00 a.m. and 5:00 p.m. on Monday, May 4, 1942, or between 9:00 a.m. and 5:00 p.m. on Tuesday, May 5, 1942.

2. Evacuees must carry with them on departure for the Assembly Center, the following property:

   (a) Bedding and linens (no mattress) for each member of the family;

   (b) Toilet articles for each member of the family;

   (c) Extra clothing for each member of the family;

   (d) Sufficient knives, forks, spoons, plates, bowls and cups for each member of the family;

   (e) Essential personal effects for each member of the family.

   All items carried will be securely packaged, tied and plainly marked with the name of the owner and numbered in accordance with instructions obtained at the Civil Control Station. The size and number of packages is limited to that which can be carried by the individual or family group.

3. No pets of any kind will be permitted.

4. No personal items and no household goods will be shipped to the Assembly Center.

5. The United States Government through its agencies will provide for the storage, at the sole risk of the owner, of the more substantial household items, such as iceboxes, washing machines, pianos and other heavy furniture. Cooking utensils and other small items will be accepted for storage if crated, packed and plainly marked with the name and address of the owner. Only one name and address will be used by a given family.

6. Each family, and individual living alone, will be furnished transportation to the Assembly Center or will be authorized to travel by private automobile in a supervised group. All instructions pertaining to the movement will be obtained at the Civil Control Station.

Go to the Civil Control Station between the hours of 8:00 a.m. and 5:00 p.m., Monday, May 4, 1942, or between the hours of 8:00 a.m. and 5:00 p.m., Tuesday, May 5, 1942, to receive further instructions.

J. L. DEWITT
Lieutenant General, U.S. Army
Commanding

SOURCE 23.3 | CHIEF JUSTICE HARLAN F. STONE, Hirabayashi v. United States *Decision* (1943)

Gordon Kiyoshi Hirabayashi, a Japanese American student at the University of Washington, was convicted in 1942 for violating a curfew and for refusing to go to a relocation camp. With the assistance of the American Civil Liberties Union, Hirabayashi took his case all the way to the U.S. Supreme Court. In his decision, Chief Justice Harlan F. Stone upheld the conviction and the constitutionality of Executive Order 9066. Hirabayashi's conviction was not overturned until 1987.

Distinctions between citizens solely because of their ancestry are, by their very nature, odious to a free people whose institutions are founded upon the doctrine of equality. For that reason, legislative classification or discrimination based on race alone has often been held to be a denial of equal protection. We may assume that these considerations would be controlling here were it not for the fact that the danger of espionage and sabotage, in time of war and of threatened invasion, calls upon the military authorities to scrutinize every relevant fact bearing on the loyalty of populations in the danger areas. Because racial discriminations are in most circumstances irrelevant, and therefore prohibited, it by no means follows that, in dealing with the perils of war, Congress and the Executive are wholly precluded from taking into account those facts and circumstances which are relevant to measures for our national defense and for the successful prosecution of the war, and which may, in fact, place citizens of one ancestry in a different category from others. . . .

The adoption by Government, in the crisis of war and of threatened invasion, of measures for the public safety, based upon the recognition of facts and circumstances which indicate that a group of one national extraction may menace that safety more than others, is not wholly beyond the limits of the Constitution, and is not to be condemned merely because, in other and in most circumstances, racial distinctions are irrelevant. Here, the aim of Congress and the Executive was the protection against sabotage of war materials and utilities in areas thought to be in danger of Japanese invasion and air attack. We have stated in detail facts and circumstances with respect to the American citizens of Japanese ancestry residing on the Pacific Coast which support the judgment of the war-waging branches of the Government that some restrictive measure was urgent. We cannot say that these facts and circumstances, considered in the particular war setting, could afford no ground for differentiating citizens of Japanese ancestry from other groups in the United States. The fact alone that attack on our shores was threatened by Japan, rather than another enemy power, set these citizens apart from others who have no particular associations with Japan.

Our investigation here does not go beyond the inquiry whether, in the light of all the relevant circumstances preceding and attending their promulgation, the challenged orders and statute afforded a reasonable basis for the action taken in

Source: *Hirabayashi v. United States*, 320 U.S. 81 (1943).

imposing the curfew. We cannot close our eyes to the fact, demonstrated by experience, that, in time of war, residents having ethnic affiliations with an invading enemy may be a greater source of danger than those of a different ancestry. Nor can we deny that Congress, and the military authorities acting with its authorization, have constitutional power to appraise the danger in the light of facts of public notoriety. We need not now attempt to define the ultimate boundaries of the war power. We decide only the issue as we have defined it—we decide only that the curfew order as applied, and at the time it was applied, was within the boundaries of the war power. In this case, it is enough that circumstances within the knowledge of those charged with the responsibility for maintaining the national defense afforded a rational basis for the decision which they made. Whether we would have made it is irrelevant.

SOURCE 23.4 | JUSTICE FRANK MURPHY, *Dissent in* Korematsu v. United States (1944)

Like Gordon Hirabayashi's case, Fred Korematsu's challenge of the constitutionality of internment camps was also denied. Not all the Supreme Court justices agreed, however. One of the dissenters in the *Korematsu* case was Justice Frank Murphy. A former governor of Michigan and a former attorney general of the United States, Murphy had established himself as a protector of civil liberties and a liberal voice on the Court. In the following excerpt from his *Korematsu* dissent, Murphy offers social and constitutional reasons for denying the legality of internment.

This exclusion of "all persons of Japanese ancestry, both alien and non-alien," from the Pacific Coast area on a plea of military necessity in the absence of martial law ought not to be approved. Such exclusion goes over "the very brink of constitutional power," and falls into the ugly abyss of racism.

In dealing with matters relating to the prosecution and progress of a war, we must accord great respect and consideration to the judgments of the military authorities who are on the scene and who have full knowledge of the military facts. The scope of their discretion must, as a matter of necessity and common sense, be wide. And their judgments ought not to be overruled lightly by those whose training and duties ill-equip them to deal intelligently with matters so vital to the physical security of the nation.

At the same time, however, it is essential that there be definite limits to military discretion, especially where martial law has not been declared. Individuals must not be left impoverished of their constitutional rights on a plea of military necessity that has neither substance nor support. Thus, like other claims conflicting with the asserted constitutional rights of the individual, the military claim must subject itself to the judicial process of having its reasonableness determined and its conflicts with other interests reconciled.

Source: *Korematsu v. United States*, 323 U.S. 214 (1944).

What are the allowable limits of military discretion, and whether or not they have been overstepped in a particular case, are judicial questions.

The judicial test of whether the Government, on a plea of military necessity, can validly deprive an individual of any of his constitutional rights is whether the deprivation is reasonably related to a public danger that is so "immediate, imminent, and impending" as not to admit of delay and not to permit the intervention of ordinary constitutional processes to alleviate the danger. Civilian Exclusion Order No. 34, banishing from a prescribed area of the Pacific Coast "all persons of Japanese ancestry, both alien and non-alien," clearly does not meet that test. Being an obvious racial discrimination, the order deprives all those within its scope of the equal protection of the laws as guaranteed by the *Fifth Amendment*. It further deprives these individuals of their constitutional rights to live and work where they will, to establish a home where they choose and to move about freely. In excommunicating them without benefit of hearings, this order also deprives them of all their constitutional rights to procedural due process. Yet no reasonable relation to an "immediate, imminent, and impending" public danger is evident to support this racial restriction, which is one of the most sweeping and complete deprivations of constitutional rights in the history of this nation in the absence of martial law. . . .

That this forced exclusion was the result in good measure of this erroneous assumption of racial guilt, rather than *bona fide* military necessity is evidenced by the Commanding General's Final Report on the evacuation from the Pacific Coast area. In it, he refers to all individuals of Japanese descent as "subversive," as belonging to "an enemy race" whose "racial strains are undiluted," and as constituting "over 112,000 potential enemies . . . at large today" along the Pacific Coast. In support of this blanket condemnation of all persons of Japanese descent, however, no reliable evidence is cited to show that such individuals were generally disloyal, or had generally so conducted themselves in this area as to constitute a special menace to defense installations or war industries, or had otherwise, by their behavior, furnished reasonable ground for their exclusion as a group. . . .

The main reasons relied upon by those responsible for the forced evacuation, therefore, do not prove a reasonable relation between the group characteristics of Japanese Americans and the dangers of invasion, sabotage and espionage. The reasons appear, instead, to be largely an accumulation of much of the misinformation, half-truths and insinuations that for years have been directed against Japanese Americans by people with racial and economic prejudices—the same people who have been among the foremost advocates of the evacuation. . . .

No one denies, of course, that there were some disloyal persons of Japanese descent on the Pacific Coast who did all in their power to aid their ancestral land. Similar disloyal activities have been engaged in by many persons of German, Italian and even more pioneer stock in our country. But to infer that examples of individual disloyalty prove group disloyalty and justify discriminatory action against the entire group is to deny that, under our system of law, individual guilt is the sole basis for deprivation of rights. Moreover, this inference, which is at the very heart of the evacuation orders, has been used in support of the abhorrent and despicable treatment of minority groups by the dictatorial tyrannies which this nation is now pledged to destroy. To give constitutional sanction to that inference in this case, however well intentioned may have been the military command on the Pacific Coast, is to adopt one of the cruelest of the rationales used by our enemies to destroy the dignity of the individual and to encourage and open the door to discriminatory actions against other minority groups in the passions of tomorrow. . . .

I dissent, therefore, from this legalization of racism. Racial discrimination in any form and in any degree has no justifiable part whatever in our democratic way of life. It is unattractive in any setting, but it is utterly revolting among a free people who have embraced the principles set forth in the Constitution of the United States. All residents of this nation are kin in some way by blood or culture to a foreign land. Yet they are primarily and necessarily a part of the new and distinct civilization of the United States. They must, accordingly, be treated at all times as the heirs of the American experiment, and as entitled to all the rights and freedoms guaranteed by the Constitution.

SOURCE 23.5 | JISHIRO MIYAUCHI, *Heart Mountain, Wyoming Internee Camp* (1943)

This painting, "Heart Mt. Wyo 1943," was made by Jishiro Miyauchi, one of the more than 10,000 Japanese American inmates at the Heart Mountain Relocation Camp in Wyoming who were interned during World War II. Most of the internees were American citizens of Japanese descent from the West Coast.

"Heart Mt. Wyo 1943" (detail), by J. Miyauchi. Reprinted by permission of Kay Yonemoto Collection and with permission from the Jishiro Miyauchi Family.

INTERPRET THE EVIDENCE

1. Why did Monica Sone think she and her friends would not be treated as Americans (Source 23.1)? Evaluate the Nisei's relationship to the United States.

2. How would you describe the government's strategy for relocating the Japanese (Source 23.2)? What hardships would Japanese people face? What assistance did the government offer to relocated people?

3. Why did Chief Justice Harlan F. Stone uphold the constitutionality of Executive Order 9066 (Source 23.3)? How does he counter arguments that a curfew for Japanese people constitutes racial discrimination?

4. Why did Justice Frank Murphy argue that internment was unconstitutional (Source 23.4)? Why, in his opinion, did the government specifically target Japanese citizens?

5. What message(s) is Jishiro Miyauchi trying to convey in his painting of the Heart Mountain internment camp (Source 23.5)?

6. How did opponents of internment invoke American values in their arguments?

PUT IT IN CONTEXT

1. In what ways was internment different from other instances when the United States suppressed civil liberties during wartime?

2. What might have been alternatives to Japanese internment?

The Korean War

▶ Analyze the Cold War assumptions that led to the Korean War.

In the late 1940s Asia became an increasingly important arena in the Cold War. The Truman administration hoped China would be a stabilizing force in the region, but its hopes were dashed when Mao Zedong's Communist troops defeated Chinese Nationalists in the fall of 1949. Truman responded by sending aid to anti-Communist forces in Burma, French Indochina, Indonesia, and other Asian nations. In South Korea, the United States lent its support to anti-Communist Syngman Rhee, while the Soviets and Chinese backed Communists in North Korea, under the leadership of Kim Il-sung (Source 24.1).

The Korean War began when Kim's forces attacked South Korea in June 1950 (Source 24.2). The Cold War's first "hot war," the conflict would prove to be a difficult test for President Truman (Source 24.3). General Douglas MacArthur, commander of U.S. and United Nations forces, frequently clashed with the president on their competing visions of the conflict (Source 24.4). The five-star general was frustrated with Truman's limited war approach. Truman, on the other hand, worried the conflict would become another world war, especially after Mao sent hundreds of thousands of Chinese troops into Korea. MacArthur's airing of those frustrations prompted Truman to forbid him from making public statements. In early April 1951, MacArthur sent a letter expressing his opinions to Congressman Joseph Martin, who then read the letter on the floor of Congress (Source 24.5). Five days later Truman replaced MacArthur with General Matthew Ridgway. Ridgway, however, wasn't any more successful than MacArthur had been. By 1952 the war's stalemate had created such a crisis for Truman that he decided not to seek reelection.

The documents in this project reveal escalating tensions in Korea and also the crisis surrounding MacArthur's public airing of his differences with Truman.

SOURCE 24.1 | SIDNEY W. SOUERS, *NSC 48* (December 1949)

By 1946 the Truman administration had settled on a Cold War policy of containment to fight the expansion of communism. While initially a strategy directed toward Europe and the Middle East, containment was also shifted to Asia after China fell to communism. The following selection, from a policy document written by the National Security Council, discusses the Cold War situation in Asia and U.S. goals in the region.

A Report to the President by the National Security Council

WASHINGTON, December 30, 1949. TOP SECRET

NSC 48/2

THE POSITION OF THE UNITED STATES WITH RESPECT TO ASIA

CONCLUSIONS

Our basic security objectives with respect to Asia[1] are:

- Development of the nations and peoples of Asia on a stable and self-sustaining basis in conformity with the purposes and principles of the United Nations Charter.

- Development of sufficient military power in selected non-Communist nations of Asia to maintain internal security and to prevent further encroachment by communism.

- Gradual reduction and eventual elimination of the preponderant power and influence of the USSR in Asia to such a degree that the Soviet Union will not be capable of threatening from that area the security of the United States or its friends and that the Soviet Union would encounter serious obstacles should it attempt to threaten the peace, national independence and stability of the Asiatic nations.

- Prevention of power relationships in Asia which would enable any other nation or alliance to threaten the security of the United States from that area, or the peace, national independence and stability of the Asiatic nations.

In pursuit of these objectives, the United States should act to:

- Support non-Communist forces in taking the initiative in Asia;

- Exert an influence to advance its own national interests; and

- Initiate action in such a manner as will appeal to the Asiatic nations as being compatible with their national interests and worthy of their support.

Source: Sidney W. Souers, Memorandum by the Executive Secretary of the National Security Council (Souers) to the National Security Council, December 30, 1949. U.S. Department of State, Office of the Historian, https://history.state.gov/historicaldocuments/frus1949v07p2/d386.

[1] For the purposes of this report "Asia" is defined as that part of the continent of Asia south of the USSR and east of Iran together with the major off-shore islands—Japan, Formosa, the Philippines, Indonesia, and Ceylon.

SOURCE 24.2 | TERENTI SHTYKOV, *Telegram* (January 19, 1950)

Kim Il-sung enjoyed Soviet support in his rise to dominance within the Korean Communist movement. Terenti Shtykov, the leader of Soviet occupation forces in North Korea, proved an especially useful ally for Kim. The following selections are from a telegram written by Shtykov to Moscow describing Kim's military and political goals for Korea.

But since Rhee Syngmann is still not instigating an attack, it means that the liberation of the people of the southern part of the country and the unification of the country are being drawn out, that he (Kim Il Sung) thinks that he needs again to visit Comrade Stalin and receive an order and permission for offensive action by the Peoples' Army for the purpose of the liberation of the people of Southern Korea. Further Kim said that he himself cannot begin an attack, because he is a communist, a disciplined person and for him the order of Comrade Stalin is law. Then he stated that if it is not possible to meet with Comrade Stalin, then he will try to meet with Mao Zedong, after his return from Moscow. Kim underscored that Mao Zedong promised to render him assistance after the conclusion of the war in China. (Apparently Kim Il Sung has in mind the conversation of his representative Kim Il with Mao Zedong in June 1949, about which I reported by ciphered telegram.) Kim said that he also has other questions for Mao Zedong, in particular the question of the possibility of the creation of an eastern bureau of the Cominform. He further stated that on all these questions he will try to meet with Comrade Shtykov and to secure through him a meeting with Comrade Stalin. . . .

I answered Kim that he has not raised the question of a meeting with Comrade Stalin and if he raises such a question, then it is possible that Comrade Stalin will receive him. On the question of an attack on the Ongjin peninsula I answered him that it is impossible to do this. Then I tried to conclude the conversation on these questions and, alluding to a later time, proposed to go home. With that the conversation was concluded.

After the luncheon Kim Il Sung was in a mood of some intoxication. It was obvious that he began this conversation not accidentally, but had thought it out earlier, with the goal of laying out his frame of mind and elucidating our attitude to these questions.

In the process of this conversation Kim Il Sung repeatedly underscored his wish to get the advice of Comrade Stalin on the question of the situation in the south of Korea, since [Kim Il Sung] is constantly nurturing his idea about an attack.

Source: "Document VI: Ciphered Telegram from Shtykov to Vyshinsky, 19 January 1950," *Cold War International History Project Bulletin*, Issue 5 (Washington, D.C.: Woodrow Wilson International Center for Scholars, 1995), 8, https://www.wilsoncenter.org/publication/bulletin-no-5-spring-1995.

SOURCE 24.3 | HARRY TRUMAN, *Radio Address on Korea* (April 11, 1951)

Douglas MacArthur's status as a war hero and charismatic military leader meant, for Truman, that disciplining him was politically risky. When the president and his advisers decided to relieve MacArthur of command, Truman sought to divert potential criticism by taking his case directly to the American people. The following is a selection from Truman's speech about MacArthur and the conflict in Korea, broadcast over national radio.

I want to talk plainly to you tonight about what we are doing in Korea and about our policy in the Far East. In the simplest terms, what we are doing in Korea is this: We are trying to prevent a third world war.

I think most people in this country recognized that fact last June. And they warmly supported the decision of the government to help the Republic of Korea against the Communist aggressors. Now, many persons, even some who applauded our decision to defend Korea, have forgotten the basic reason for our action.

It is right for us to be in Korea. It was right last June. It is right today. I want to remind you why this is true. . . .

But you may ask: . . . Why don't we bomb Manchuria and China itself? Why don't we assist Chinese Nationalist troops to land on the mainland of China?

If we were to do these things we would be running a very grave risk of starting a general war. If that were to happen, we would have brought about the exact situation we are trying to prevent. If we were to do these things, we would become entangled in a vast conflict on the continent of Asia and our task would become immeasurably more difficult all over the world.

What would suit the ambitions of the Kremlin better than for our military forces to be committed to a full-scale war with Red China?

It may well be that, in spite of our best efforts, the Communists may spread the war. But it would be wrong—tragically wrong—for us to take the initiative in extending the war. . . .

A number of events have made it evident that General MacArthur did not agree with that policy. I have therefore considered it essential to relieve General MacArthur so that there would be no doubt or confusion as to the real purpose and aim of our policy. It was with the deepest personal regret that I found myself compelled to take this action. General MacArthur is one of our greatest military commanders. But the cause of world peace is more important than any individual.

Source: *Department of State Bulletin*, XXIV (April 16, 1951), 603–5.

SOURCE 24.4 | DOUGLAS MACARTHUR, *Speech before Congress* (April 19, 1951)

When MacArthur returned to the United States, he was given a hero's welcome, including a ticker tape parade in New York City. He also made a speech before the U.S. Congress in which he explained his side of the conflict with Truman. The following excerpt is from the end of that speech.

But once war is forced upon us, there is no other alternative than to apply every available means to bring it to a swift end. War's very object is victory, not prolonged indecision.

In war there can be no substitute for victory.

There are some who for varying reasons would appease Red China. They are blind to history's clear lesson, for history teaches with unmistakable emphasis that appeasement but begets new and bloodier wars. . . .

The tragedy of Korea is further heightened by the fact that its military action was confined to its territorial limits. It condemns that nation, which it is our purpose to save, to suffer the devastating impact of full naval and air bombardment while the enemy's sanctuaries are fully protected from such attack and devastation.

Of the nations of the world, Korea alone, up to now, is the sole one which has risked its all against communism. . . .

I am closing my 52 years of military service. When I joined the Army, even before the turn of the century, it was the fulfillment of all my boyish hopes and dreams. The world has turned over many times since I took the oath at West Point, and the hopes and dreams have all since vanished, but I still remember the refrain of one of the most popular barracks ballads of that day which proclaimed most proudly that old soldiers never die; they just fade away. And like the old soldier of that ballad, I now close my military career and just fade away, an old soldier who tried to do his duty as God gave him the light to see that duty.

Source: *Congressional Record*, XCVII (April 19, 1951), 4124–25, http://www.pbs.org/wgbh/amex/macarthur/filmmore/reference/primary/macspeech05.html.

SOURCE 24.5 | HERBERT BLOCK, *"We've Been Using More of a Roundish One,"* Washington Post (May 1951)

Truman's firing of MacArthur brought him widespread condemnation in the press and the American public. Unusual, then, is the following political cartoon, which criticizes MacArthur's vision of the Korean War. Created by the Pulitzer Prize–winning editorial cartoonist Herb Block, it was published by the *Washington Post* only weeks after MacArthur's firing.

A 1951 Herblock Cartoon, © The Herb Block Foundation

INTERPRET THE EVIDENCE

1. What roles does the National Security Council believe the Soviet Union plays in the spread of communism (Source 24.1)? What are the council's suggestions for containing communism in Asia?

2. What is Kim Il-sung asking of the Soviet Union, and why (Source 24.2)? How does Kim envision the international Communist movement? Why do you think he tells Shtykov he will meet with Mao if he cannot meet with Stalin?

3. According to Truman (Source 24.3), in what ways were MacArthur's recommendations for fighting the war at odds with the reasons for being in Korea in the first place? How did he characterize MacArthur's actions?

4. Why did MacArthur accuse Truman of appeasing China (Source 24.4)? In what ways does MacArthur's speech highlight the differences between the political and military goals of the Korean War?

5. Why would Herbert Block's cartoon (Source 24.5) depict Secretary of Defense George Marshall instead of President Truman? What parts of the world appear on each globe, and what do these differences signify? Why does MacArthur's globe have a button on it?

PUT IT IN CONTEXT

1. Why were MacArthur's actions considered a threat to the civilian leadership of the military?

2. What about the conflict in Korea turned it into a large-scale war in the early stages of the Cold War?

The Postwar Suburbs

▶ Compare the differences between the ideal and the reality of post–World War II suburbanization in the U.S.

After the Second World War, the nation's culture, politics, and society changed in many ways. Perhaps nowhere were these changes more clearly on display than in the burgeoning suburbs. Millions of Americans fled cities to find new homes and new jobs in suburban areas, especially in the Sun Belt states of the West and South. By the end of the 1950s, one-third of the nation's population lived in suburbs.

Images of suburbia proliferated throughout American culture. Advertisements promised Americans who relocated to these new developments that they could enjoy tree-lined streets, neat (if small) houses, freshly cut lawns, and lives free of worry, poverty, and crime. Yet the actual history of suburbia is far more complex. A number of interests converged in these new communities (Sources 25.1 and 25.2). Home builders sought to build as many houses as quickly as possible and to ensure that their developments fit the ideal of the suburban dream. This meant both targeted marketing and the exclusion of racial minorities. The federal government provided low-interest loans through the Federal Housing Administration and GI Bill and constructed roads to connect the suburbs to cities. Cars, service stations, and hotels all became a part of the national landscape.

Great numbers of Americans had little access to this suburban dream. Low-income residents could not afford to buy new homes, and developers typically prevented African Americans and other minorities from moving to suburban communities (Source 25.5). Women found themselves consigned to lives of domestic labor and child care—an issue feminist Betty Friedan later called "the problem that has no name." Many men spent nearly as much time in traffic as they did with their families (Sources 25.3 and 25.4).

The following documents and transcripts illuminate the tactics that people and businesses used to lure urban dwellers to the suburbs. They also explore positive and negative aspects of the country's increasing suburbanization.

SOURCE 25.1 | Metropolitan Highway Construction: Boston *Transcript* (1955)

Suburbanization could not have occurred to such a dramatic degree without automobiles and the construction of new roads that allowed commuters to travel from the suburbs to the city for work. The Ford Motor Company produced a film to muster support for the extension of Route 128, a highway designed to bypass the traffic of downtown Boston.

00:00:00

MAN 1: Boston is the hub of a very complex highway system. In New England, all roads lead to Boston and Boston has kept growing, swelling the towns around it. Today its metropolitan area extends over 42 cities and towns, with a population of two and one half million.

Once country roads served the outlying communities adequately. But overnight they became city streets, with through traffic hopelessly entangled as you see it here.

00:00:32

It became so bad that a trip of 15 miles, say from Stoneham, north of Boston, to Newton on the south side, actually took over an hour. At the state house, there was a highway on paper, which could have alleviated all that traffic congestion. Lack of public support had kept it in the files, until the people of Essex County, through their board of trade, got it out into the light of day.

00:00:59

Here you see it on the map, Highway 128. Starting from Gloucester, the old fishing point, it swings in a wide 18 mile arc, around the rim of greater Boston, all the way down to Dedham, with its last section now nearing completion.

Today, John Smith of Gloucester can leave his family in the morning and travel safely and quickly over a modern express highway to his job. Because new roads, like magic arteries, pump increased values into adjacent land, he now travels past property whose value has increased 100 times over.

00:01:36

Along this highway have sprouted seven great industrial centers, occupied by some of the country's leading manufacturers, and other centers are now being developed. New wealth and new revenues have come to the old New England towns along the highway.

00:01:56

And not to forget our Mr. Smith, and thousands more like him, here he is arriving at his place of work without once having had to fight the Boston traffic.

MAN 1: When the people of Essex County pushed for the construction of 128, in order to relieve traffic congestion, they didn't know they were going to ring Boston with a golden semicircle. And that's what Highway 128 is called today, "Boston's Golden Semicircle."

00:02:23

So far you've seen what improved highways and traffic control mean to a metropolitan area. But all good roads are part of one great pattern, the interstate system that serves the whole nation, the great primary roads that connect the cities, and then the roads that feed into the system. We need good secondary roads to serve the rural population and small towns of America.

SOURCE 25.2 | In the Suburbs *Transcript* (1957)

Automobile companies were not the only industry to promote suburbanization. Magazines such as *Redbook* also capitalized on the growing suburban market. *Redbook* produced a film that portrayed the joys of suburban living, in hopes of attracting advertisers. The transcript follows.

00:00:00

VOICEOVER: The suburbs. Almost as much written about as Madison Avenue, and just as much in need of reflection.
[sounds of children playing]
Like Madison Avenue, life in the suburbs has its good moments and others not so good.
[funny music]

00:00:30

WOMAN 1: Oh no.
MAN 1: Oh.
VOICEOVER: Discouraged? Disgruntled? Heck no. They're glad to be here. Remember?
[creepy music]

00:00:59

[cheerful music]
VOICEOVER: And so they joined the stream of family life in the suburbs, soon to become part of its familiar sight. Soon to absorb its familiar sounds.

00:01:29

[door closing]
MAN 2: Anybody home?

[child whistling]
[child humming]
[laughter]

00:02:04

[cheerful music]
VOICEOVER: These are what Redbook means by its young adults: people in a certain living situation with particular interests and particular goals.

00:02:31

VOICEOVER: These young adults begin to discover Redbook about the time they apply for their marriage license, start life in their own homes, have their first baby, take out their first loan, and they stay with Redbook through their busiest years.
As Redbook sees them, they are an energetic lot, a carefree lot, even though so suddenly plunged into family life. As the babies start coming, they usually decide to concentrate on their houses, with the woman staying home to learn new ways to run a household. . . .

00:03:06

[dramatic music]
VOICEOVER: Where it soon dawns on here that she could use a little expert help. While the kids are young, many of the mothers try to stay at home, which isn't always so easy either.
[child and dog noises]

00:03:33

[child screaming inaudibly]

SOURCE 25.3 | HARRY HENDERSON, *The Mass-Produced Suburbs* (1953)

The advantages and drawbacks of postwar suburbanization fueled debate among social critics and journalists. Harry Henderson began investigating suburban life in 1950 to determine the social effect of suburban living. The following excerpt from an article published in *Harper's* reveals Henderson's opinions on several aspects of suburban life, including home ownership, family life, crime, and community.

Source: Harry Henderson, "The Mass-Produced Suburbs," *Harper's Magazine*, November 1953, 25–32.

At first glance, regardless of variations in trim, color, and position of the houses, they seem monotonous; nothing rises above two stories, there are no full-grown trees, and the horizon is an endless picket fence of telephone poles and television aerials. (The mass builder seeks flat land because it cuts his construction costs.)

However one may feel about it aesthetically, this puts the emphasis on people and their activities. One rarely hears complaints about the identical character of the houses. "You don't feel it when you live here," most people say. One mother, a Midwestern college graduate with two children, told me: "We're not peas in a pod. I thought it would be like that, especially because incomes are nearly the same. But it's amazing how different and varied people are, likes and dislikes, attitude and wants. I never really knew what people were like until I came here."

Since no one can acquire prestige through an imposing house, or inherited position, activity—the participation in community or group affairs—becomes the basis of prestige. In addition, it is the quickest way to meet people and make friends. In communities of strangers, where everybody realizes his need for companionship, the first year is apt to witness almost frantic participation in all kinds of activities. Later, as friends are made, this tapers off somewhat. . . .

For the women this is a long, monotonous daily proposition. Generally the men, once home, do not want to leave. They want to "relax" or "improve the property"—putter around the lawn or shrubbery. However, the women want a "change." Thus, groups of women often go to the movies together.

Usually both husband and wife are involved in some group activity and have meetings to go to. A frequent complaint is: "We never get time to see each other"; or, "We merely pass coming and going." On the one occasion when I was refused an interview, the husband said, "Gee, I'd like to help, but I so seldom get a chance to see my wife for a whole evening. . . . I'd rather not have the interruption."

Many couples credit television, which simultaneously eased baby-sitting, entertainment, and financial problems, with having brought them closer. Their favorites are comedy shows, especially those about young couples, such as *I Love Lucy*. Though often contemptuous of many programs, they speak of TV gratefully as "something we can share," as "bringing the romance back." . . .

Crime in Suburbia

Even Levittown, with 70,000 people not far from New York's turbulent, scheming underworld, has virtually no crime. According to the Nassau County police, who studied one year's record, it had no murders, robberies, or auto thefts during that period; an average city of that size during the same period would have had 4 murders, 3 robberies, and 149 auto thefts. . . .

Police attribute this lack of crime to the fact that nearly all the men were honorably discharged from the armed services and subjected to a credit screening. This, they say, "eliminated the criminal element and riff-raff." Some police officials included the absence of slums and disreputable hang-outs as causes. Personally, I felt many more factors were involved, including the absence of real poverty; the strong ties of family, religious, and organizational activities; steady employment; and the absence of a restrictive, frustrating social structure. . . .

Socially, the outstanding characteristic of these people is their friendliness, warmth, and lack of pretentious snobbery. Outgoing and buoyant, they are quick to recognize common problems and the need for co-operation, one does not find the indifference, coldness, and "closed doors" of a long-established community. There is much casual "dropping in" and visiting from house to house which results in the sharing of many problems and pleasures. Often the discussion of a few women over supper plans will end up with four or five families eating together. This may then lead to "fun," which may be anything from cards to "just talk" or "everybody trying to roller-skate, acting like a bunch of kids." Nobody goes "out" often. Many report that, as a result of this pattern of living, they "drink more often but get high less" than they used to. Drinking, it seemed to me, had become much more of a social amenity and less of an emotional safety valve than it is elsewhere.

SOURCE 25.4 | MALVINA REYNOLDS, *Little Boxes* (1962)

Singer, songwriter, and activist Malvina Reynolds watched firsthand as new suburbs sprouted around her hometown of San Francisco. She wrote the following song, "Little Boxes," about Daly City, a community of tract housing developed by Henry Doelger. Folksinger Pete Seeger's version of the song was a hit in 1963, and its message continues to find an audience. Reynolds's version was featured as the theme song to the Showtime television series *Weeds*.

Little boxes on the hillside,
Little boxes made of ticky tacky,
Little boxes on the hillside,
Little boxes all the same.
There's a green one and a pink one
And a blue one and a yellow one,
And they're all made out of ticky tacky
And they all look just the same.

And the people in the houses
All went to the university,
Where they were put in boxes
And they came out all the same,
And there's doctors and lawyers,
And business executives,
And they're all made out of ticky tacky
And they all look just the same.

Source: Malvina Reynolds, *Little Boxes and Other Handmade Songs* (New York: Oak Publications, 1964), 28–29.

And they all play on the golf course
And drink their martinis dry,
And they all have pretty children
And the children go to school,
And the children go to summer camp
And then to the university,
Where they are put in boxes
And they come out all the same.

And the boys go into business
And marry and raise a family
In boxes made of ticky tacky
And they all look just the same.
There's a green one and a pink one
And a blue one and a yellow one,
And they're all made out of ticky tacky
And they all look just the same.

SOURCE 25.5 | JACKIE ROBINSON, *Testimony before the United States Commission on Civil Rights* (1959)

Even though the Supreme Court outlawed restrictive covenants in its 1948 *Shelley v. Kraemer* decision, African Americans still faced often-insurmountable hurdles when they attempted to buy homes in new suburbs. As the first African American baseball player in the major leagues, Jackie Robinson made history by crossing color lines. Yet even someone of Robinson's fame and stature had difficulty buying a suburban home. In the following testimony before the United States Commission on Civil Rights, Robinson relates his experience and argues for change.

When my wife and I decided to move from St. Albans, Long Island [ca. 1956], we were put through the usual bag of tricks right in this State. At first we were told the house we were interested in had been sold just before we inquired, or we would be invited to make an offer, a sort of a sealed bid, and then we'd be told that offers higher than ours had been turned down. Then we tried buying houses on the spot for whatever price was asked. They handled this by telling us the house had been taken off the market. Once we met a broker who told us he would like to help us find a home, but his clients were against selling to Negroes. Whether or not we got a story with the refusal, the results were always the same. Because of these tactics, we began to look in Connecticut; and we finally were able to settle in Stamford due to the strong efforts of some very wonderful people there.

Source: U.S. Commission on Civil Rights, *Hearings before the United States Commission on Civil Rights: Housing*, vol. 1, *Hearings Held in New York, February 2–3, 1959* (Washington, D.C.: Government Printing Office, 1959), 271.

Now, this leads to a basic truth about ending segregation in housing, as in any other phase of our life: That is, Government regulations alone are not enough. Public housing operated on an open-occupancy basis by itself is not enough. True, we need both of these; but we also need positive action by individuals to spur bias-free, privately built housing.

I went to Washington about 10 times in recent years to confer with officials, seeking action which would grant Negroes some progress toward equal rights in housing. The officials have been very polite to me but, regardless of the reason, nothing has been done.

In the 25 years that the FHA [Federal Housing Administration] has been in existence a grand total of some 200,000 dwelling units available to Negroes have been built with FHA assistance. Meanwhile, builders have constructed a million units a year or better for quite a while. Now, 200,000 units may sound like quite a bit of housing, but it is a tiny fraction compared with the 25-year total of housing built with FHA aid. FHA is not necessarily at fault. It is just that hardly anyone has built private housing open to Negroes until very recently.

We use such words as "discrimination" and "equality," but they don't tell the story.

There is a builder in New York whose conscience was troubled about housing discrimination against Negroes. Nevertheless, he was afraid that if he would let just one Negro buy a home it would spoil his business success. So, with a guilty conscience, he stalled a Negro buyer for just about a year and a half. Things came to a head when the Negro broke into tears in the builder's office and left. The builder said, "If he had waited just another minute, I would have sold him the house." The builder now sells to Negroes, but he had to first feel some measure of the harm that he was working on another human being.

We know that for many charity begins at home. So do hate, hostility, and delinquency, especially when the home environment is a slum, lacking adequate space, lacking facilities, but not lacking for high rentals, while infested with insects and rodents. . . .

Because of discrimination in housing, the end result for many is mental and physical suffering, ofttimes personal tragedy, domestic difficulties, discouragement, a waste of human potential, and, finally, an abundance of community problems.

INTERPRET THE EVIDENCE

1. Why would the Ford Motor Company favor expanding Route 128 (Source 25.1)? What benefits of expanding the highway are explained in this transcript? What potential hazards are left out?

2. How does the *Redbook* film depict suburban life (Source 25.2)? How does it portray life in the city? What are the "particular interests and particular goals" of the "young adults" of the suburbs? Who seems to be left out of this story?

3. How would you describe Harry Henderson's view of the suburbs (Source 25.3)? What advantages does he identify? What are the potential negatives of suburban living?

4. How does Malvina Reynolds describe the suburbs (Source 25.4)? Do you think she would have agreed with Harry Henderson's assessment of suburban life? Why or why not? Who do you think was the intended audience for this song?

5. According to Jackie Robinson, why did most suburban developments remain racially homogeneous (Source 25.5)? What does Robinson propose as a solution to this problem?

PUT IT IN CONTEXT

1. What economic, social, and political forces encouraged the growth of the suburbs in the 1950s?

Debating the Vietnam War

▶ Explain and evaluate the domestic and international political concerns that shaped the Johnson Administration's actions in Vietnam and how President Johnson's waging of the war influenced Americans' views of their government.

After John F. Kennedy's assassination in November 1963, President Lyndon Johnson was faced with a number of simmering domestic and international crises. One of these was the conflict in Vietnam. The United States had been involved in Vietnam since 1946, when President Truman decided to support the French in their attempt to regain their colony after World War II. American involvement deepened ten years later, after the French withdrew and the United States, first under President Eisenhower and then President Kennedy, became the sole sponsor of an anti-Communist South Vietnam.

Upon assuming the presidency, Johnson inherited a decades-long commitment to defeating communism in Vietnam, but one that was not yet an American war. He and his advisers feared abandoning American obligations but knew they supported a corrupt and unpopular regime (Source 26.1). Throughout the spring and summer of 1964, the president weighed his options. By the end of that summer Congress had granted Johnson the authority to fight North Vietnam as he saw fit. It would take another year before Johnson ordered significant ground forces to the south, turning the conflict into a full-scale war. The Vietnam War would be the undoing of Johnson's presidency and the cause of deep fissures in American society over its moral and military leadership in the Cold War (Source 26.2).

The following documents show the escalation of the conflict and opposition from different voices in American society (Sources 26.4 and 26.5).

SOURCE 26.1 | *Telephone Conversations between Lyndon Johnson and Senator Richard Russell (May 27, 1964)*

In his public statements about Vietnam, Johnson appeared resolute and confident, but privately he expressed great doubts to his advisers. In early summer 1964 Johnson called his friend and mentor Georgia senator Richard Russell to ask his advice. A selection from that conversation appears here, revealing Russell's opinions and also Johnson's conflicted thoughts about further involvement. One sticking point Johnson discusses is the 1954 South East Asia Treaty Organization, which required the United States and other signatories to aid any government under threat by communism.

SENATOR RUSSELL: Pretty Good. How are you Mr. President?

PRESIDENT JOHNSON: Oh, I've got lots of trouble. I want to see what you . . .

RUSSELL: Well, we all have those.

JOHNSON: What do you think about this Vietnam thing? I'd like to hear you talk a little bit.

RUSSELL: Well, frankly, Mr. President, if you were to tell me that I was authorized to settle as I saw fit, I would respectfully decline to undertake it. It's the damn worse mess that I ever saw, and I don't like to brag and I never have been right many times in my life, but I knew that we were gone [*sic*] to get into this sort of mess when we went in there. And I don't see how we're ever going to get out of it without fighting a major war with the Chinese and all of them down there in those rice paddies and jungles. I just don't see it. I just don't know what to do.

JOHNSON: Well, that's the way I have been feeling for six months.

RUSSELL: Our position is deteriorating and it looks like the more we try to do for them, the less they are willing to do for themselves. It's just a sad situation. There is no sense of responsibility there on the part of any of their leaders apparently. It is all just through generations or even centuries that they have just thought about the individual and glorified the individual. That's the only utilization of power, just to glorify the individual and not to save the state or help other people. And they just can't shed themselves of that complex. It's a hell of a situation. It is a mess, and it's going to get worse, and I don't know how or what to do. I don't think the American people are quite ready for us to send our troops in there to do the fighting. If it came down to an option of just sending the Americans in there to do the fighting, which will, of course, eventually end in a ground war or a conventional war with China, and we do them a favor every time we kill a coolie, whereas when one of our people got killed it would be a loss to us, and if it got down to that—of just pulling out—I'd get out. But then I don't know. There is undoubtedly some middle

Source: U.S. Department of State, Office of the Historian, *Foreign Relations of the United States 1964–1968*, Volume XXVII, Mainland Southeast Asia; Regional Affairs (Washington, D.C.: Government Printing Office, 2000), Document Number 52.

ground somewhere. If I was going to get out, I'd get the same crowd that got rid of old Diem to get rid of these people and to get some fellow in there that said we wish to hell we would get out. That would give us a good excuse for getting out. I see no terminal date, boy oh boy, any part of that in there.

JOHNSON: How important is it to us?

RUSSELL: It isn't important a damn bit for all this new missile stuff.

JOHNSON: I guess it is important.

RUSSELL: From a psychological standpoint.

JOHNSON: I mean, yes, and from the standpoint that we are a party to a treaty. And if we don't pay any attention to this treaty I don't guess that they think paying attention to any of them.

RUSSELL: Yeah, but we are the only ones paying attention to it.

JOHNSON: Yeah, I think that is right.

RUSSELL: You see the other people are just as bound to that treaty as we are.

JOHNSON: Yes, that's right.

RUSSELL: I think there are some twelve or fourteen other countries. . . .

JOHNSON: Well, I spend all my days with Rusk and McNamara and Bundy and Harriman and Vance, and all those folks that are dealing with it and I would say that it pretty well adds up to them now that we have got [to] show some power and some force and that they do not—they are kind of like MacArthur in Korea—they don't believe that the Chinese Communists will come into this thing. But they don't know, and nobody can really be sure, but their feeling is that they won't, and in any event, we haven't got much choice. That we are treaty bound, that we are there, this will be a domino that will kick off a whole list of others, and that we have just got to prepare for the worst. Now I have avoided that for a few days. I don't think the American people are for it. I don't agree with [Oregon senator Wayne] Morse and all that he says, but . . .

RUSSELL: Neither do I, but he is voicing the sentiment of a hell of a lot of people.

JOHNSON: I'm afraid that's right. I'm afraid that's right. I don't think the people of this country know much about Vietnam, and I don't think that they care a hell of a lot less.

SOURCE 26.2 | LYNDON JOHNSON, *"Peace without Conquest" Speech at Johns Hopkins University* (April 7, 1965)

In March 1965 the United States began Operation Rolling Thunder, an intensive bombing campaign against North Vietnam. The next month Johnson gave his first major address on the conflict, televised from Johns Hopkins University. His speech, excerpted here, was meant to explain American interests in Vietnam and, partly, to silence growing dissatisfaction with the expanding war operation.

Source: *Public Papers of the Presidents of the United States: Lyndon B. Johnson, 1965*, Volume I, entry 172 (Washington, D.C.: Government Printing Office, 1966), 394–99.

Mr. Garland, Senator Brewster, Senator Tydings, Members of the congressional delegation, members of the faculty of Johns Hopkins, student body, my fellow Americans:

Last week 17 nations sent their views to some two dozen countries having an interest in southeast Asia. We are joining those 17 countries and stating our American policy tonight which we believe will contribute toward peace in this area of the world.

I have come here to review once again with my own people the views of the American Government.

Tonight Americans and Asians are dying for a world where each people may choose its own path to change.

This is the principle for which our ancestors fought in the valleys of Pennsylvania. It is the principle for which our sons fight tonight in the jungles of Viet-Nam.

Viet-Nam is far away from this quiet campus. We have no territory there, nor do we seek any. The war is dirty and brutal and difficult. And some 400 young men, born into an America that is bursting with opportunity and promise, have ended their lives on Viet-Nam's steaming soil.

Why must we take this painful road?

Why must this Nation hazard its ease, and its interest, and its power for the sake of a people so far away?

We fight because we must fight if we are to live in a world where every country can shape its own destiny. And only in such a world will our own freedom be finally secure.

This kind of world will never be built by bombs or bullets. Yet the infirmities of man are such that force must often precede reason, and the waste of war, the works of peace.

We wish that this were not so. But we must deal with the world as it is, if it is ever to be as we wish.

The world as it is in Asia is not a serene or peaceful place.

The first reality is that North Viet-Nam has attacked the independent nation of South Viet-Nam. Its object is total conquest.

Of course, some of the people of South Viet-Nam are participating in attack on their own government. But trained men and supplies, orders and arms, flow in a constant stream from north to south.

This support is the heartbeat of the war.

And it is a war of unparalleled brutality. Simple farmers are the targets of assassination and kidnapping. Women and children are strangled in the night because their men are loyal to their government. And helpless villages are ravaged by sneak attacks. Large-scale raids are conducted on towns, and terror strikes in the heart of cities.

The confused nature of this conflict cannot mask the fact that it is the new face of an old enemy.

Over this war—and all Asia—is another reality: the deepening shadow of Communist China. The rulers in Hanoi are urged on by Peking. This is a regime which has destroyed freedom in Tibet, which has attacked India, and has been condemned by the United Nations for aggression in Korea. It is a nation which is helping the forces of violence in almost every continent. The contest in Viet-Nam is part of a wider pattern of aggressive purposes.

Why are these realities our concern? Why are we in South Viet-Nam?

We are there because we have a promise to keep. Since 1954 every American President has offered support to the people of South Viet-Nam. We have helped to build, and we have helped to defend. Thus, over many years, we have made a national pledge to help South Viet-Nam defend its independence.

And I intend to keep that promise.

To dishonor that pledge, to abandon this small and brave nation to its enemies, and to the terror that must follow, would be an unforgivable wrong.

We are also there to strengthen world order. Around the globe, from Berlin to Thailand, are people whose well-being rests, in part, on the belief that they can count on us if they are attacked. To leave Viet-Nam to its fate would shake the confidence of all these people in the value of an American commitment and in the value of America's word. The result would be increased unrest and instability, and even wider war.

We are also there because there are great stakes in the balance. Let no one think for a moment that retreat from Viet-Nam would bring an end to conflict. The battle would be renewed in one country and then another. The central lesson of our time is that the appetite of aggression is never satisfied. To withdraw from one battlefield means only to prepare for the next. We must say in southeast Asia—as we did in Europe—in the words of the Bible: "Hitherto shalt thou come, but no further."

There are those who say that all our effort there will be futile—that China's power is such that it is bound to dominate all southeast Asia. But there is no end to that argument until all of the nations of Asia are swallowed up.

There are those who wonder why we have a responsibility there. Well, we have it there for the same reason that we have a responsibility for the defense of Europe. World War II was fought in both Europe and Asia, and when it ended we found ourselves with continued responsibility for the defense of freedom.

Our objective is the independence of South Viet-Nam, and its freedom from attack. We want nothing for ourselves—only that the people of South Viet-Nam be allowed to guide their own country in their own way.

We will do everything necessary to reach that objective. And we will do only what is absolutely necessary.

SOURCE 26.3 | HERBERT BLOCK, *"Our Position Hasn't Changed at All,"* Washington Post (June 17, 1965)

In June 1965, as Johnson assured the American people that there was no change in his strategy, the Department of Defense announced it was sending 20,000 new troops to Vietnam. In response, the award-winning editorial cartoonist Herbert Block published the following cartoon questioning Johnson's credibility. A month after the cartoon's release, Johnson ordered 125,000 additional American troops to South Vietnam, turning the conflict into a large-scale ground war.

A 1965 Herblock Cartoon, © The Herb Block Foundation

SOURCE 26.4 | STUDENT NONVIOLENT COORDINATING COMMITTEE, *Statement on Vietnam* (January 6, 1966)

The Student Nonviolent Coordinating Committee (SNCC) was one of the most active civil rights organizations of the 1960s. Emerging out of the lunch counter sit-ins in the South, it consisted of student activists who pushed the civil rights movement in a younger and more radical direction. As the Vietnam War intensified, SNCC became one of the first groups to add antiwar activism to its civil rights agenda. The statement included here demonstrates the merging of SNCC's critique of American racism with its critique of America's military presence in Vietnam.

The Student Nonviolent Coordinating Committee has a right and a responsibility to dissent with United States foreign policy on any issue when it sees fit. The Student Nonviolent Coordinating Committee now states its opposition to the United States' involvement in Vietnam on these grounds:

We believe the United States government has been deceptive in its claims of concern for the freedom of the Vietnamese people, just as the government has been deceptive in claiming concern for the freedom of colored people in other countries as the Dominican Republic, the Congo, South Africa, Rhodesia, and in the United States itself.

We, the Student Nonviolent Coordinating Committee, have been involved in the black peoples' struggle for liberation and self-determination in this country for the past five years. Our work, particularly in the South, has taught us that the United States government has never guaranteed the freedom of oppressed citizens, and is not yet truly determined to end the rule of terror and oppression within its own borders.

We ourselves have often been victims of violence and confinement executed by United States governmental officials. We recall the numerous persons who have been murdered in the South because of their efforts to secure their civil and human rights, and whose murderers have been allowed to escape penalty for their crimes.

The murder of Samuel Young in Tuskegee, Alabama, is no different than the murder of peasants in Vietnam, for both Young and the Vietnamese sought, and are seeking, to secure the rights guaranteed them by law. In each case, the United States government bears a great part of the responsibility for these deaths.

Samuel Young was murdered because United States law is not being enforced. Vietnamese are murdered because the United States is pursuing an aggressive policy in violation of international law. The United States is no respecter of persons or law when such persons or laws run counter to its needs or desires.

We recall the indifference, suspicion and outright hostility with which our reports of violence have been met in the past by government officials.

Source: Student Nonviolent Coordinating Committee Statement on Vietnam, January 6, 1966, The Civil Rights Movement Veterans Website, http://www.crmvet.org/docs/snccviet.htm.

We know that for the most part, elections in this country, in the North as well as the South, are not free. We have seen that the 1965 Voting Rights Act and the 1964 Civil Rights Act have not yet been implemented with full federal power and sincerity.

We question, then, the ability and even the desire of the United States government to guarantee free elections abroad. We maintain that our country's cry of "preserve freedom in the world" is a hypocritical mask, behind which it squashes liberation movements which are not bound, and refuse to be bound, by the expediencies of United States cold war policies.

We are in sympathy with, and support, the men in this country who are unwilling to respond to a military draft which would compel them to contribute their lives to United States aggression in Vietnam in the name of the "freedom" we find so false in this country.

We recoil with horror at the inconsistency of a supposedly "free" society where responsibility to freedom is equated with the responsibility to lend oneself to military aggression. We take note of the fact that 16% of the draftees from this country are Negroes called on to stifle the liberation of Vietnam, to preserve a "democracy" which does not exist for them at home.

We ask, where is the draft for the freedom fight in the United States?

We therefore encourage those Americans who prefer to use their energy in building democratic forms within this country. We believe that work in the civil rights movement and with other human relations organizations is a valid alternative to the draft. We urge all Americans to seek this alternative, knowing full well that it may cost them their lives—as painfully as in Vietnam.

SOURCE 26.5 | ROBERT F. KENNEDY, *Vietnam Illusions* (February 8, 1968)

On January 30, 1968, Vietnamese Communists launched major offensives against cities and U.S. strongholds throughout the South. The Tet Offensive, as it was called, dealt a major blow to public support for the Vietnam War and Johnson's administration. A week after Tet, Senator Robert Kennedy delivered an impassioned antiwar speech in Chicago. Already a vocal critic of Johnson's handling of the war, Kennedy would announce his presidential candidacy a month later, a direct challenge to the sitting president.

There is an American interest in South Vietnam. We have an interest in maintaining the strength of our commitments—and surely we have demonstrated that. With all the lives and resources we have poured into Vietnam, is there anyone to argue that a government with any support from its people, with any competence to rule, with any determination to defend itself, would not long ago have been victorious over any insurgent movement, however assisted from outside its borders?

And we have another, more immediate interest: to protect the lives of our gallant young men and to conserve American resources. But we do not have an

Source: *Chicago Sun-Times*, February 11, 1968.

interest in the survival of a privileged class, growing ever more wealthy from the corruption of war, which after all our sacrifices on their behalf can ask why Vietnamese boys have to fight for Americans.

The fifth illusion is that this war can be settled in our own way and in our own time on our own terms. Such a settlement is the privilege of the triumphant, of those who crush their enemies in battle or wear away their will to fight. We simply have not done this, nor is there any prospect we will achieve such a victory.

For twenty years, first the French and then the United States have been predicting victory in Vietnam. In 1961 and in 1962, as well as 1966 and 1967, we have been told that "the tide is turning"; "there is 'light at the end of the tunnel' "; "we can soon bring home the troops—victory is near—the enemy is tiring." Once, in 1962, I participated in such predictions myself. But for twenty years we have been wrong.

The history of conflict among nations does not record another such lengthy and consistent chronicle of error as we have shown in Vietnam. It is time to discard so proven a fallacy and face the reality that a military victory is not in sight and that it probably will never come.

Unable to defeat our enemy or break his will—at least without a huge, long, and ever more costly effort—we must actively seek a peaceful settlement. We can no longer harden our terms every time Hanoi indicates it may be prepared to negotiate; and we must be willing to foresee a settlement which will give the Viet Cong and the National Liberation Front a chance to participate in the political life of the country. Not because we want them to but because that is the only way in which this struggle can be settled.

No one knows if negotiations will bring a peaceful settlement, but we do know there will be no peaceful settlement without negotiations. Nor can we have these negotiations just on our own terms. Again, we might like that. We may have to make concessions and take risks, and surely we will have to negotiate directly with the NLF as well as Hanoi. Surely it is only another illusion that still denies this basic necessity. What we must not do is confuse the prestige staked on a particular policy with the interest of the United States; nor should we be unwilling to take risks for peace when we are willing to risk so many lives in war.

INTERPRET THE EVIDENCE

1. What are Senator Richard Russell's reservations about a deeper commitment in Vietnam (Source 26.1)? Why does President Johnson feel the United States has to maintain its presence there? What role does Vietnam play in the larger international Cold War?

2. How does President Johnson try to generate sympathy for the South Vietnamese (Source 26.2)? What criticism is he responding to, and how does he address those concerns?

3. What argument is Herbert Block making about the Johnson administration (Source 26.3)? What does the cartoon suggest about President Johnson's feelings about the war?

4. How do SNCC activists compare their civil rights struggle with the struggle for freedom in Vietnam (Source 26.4)? In what ways do they charge the government with hypocrisy? On what grounds do they argue that the United States should get out of Vietnam?

5. Why would Robert Kennedy admit that he had been wrong about the conflict in Vietnam in 1962 (Source 26.5)? Does he believe it is possible to win in Vietnam? How does he characterize the South Vietnamese government?

PUT IT IN CONTEXT

1. Why did the Vietnam War lead the American people to distrust their government? How did the war shape how Americans understood the Cold War?

Women's Liberation

▶ Compare and contrast the various approaches taken by feminists, and explain why the women's liberation movement was so controversial.

Calls for women's rights attracted widespread attention during the 1960s. For many women, however, author and activist Betty Friedan's analysis of "the problem with no name" and the National Organization of Women's emphasis on legal reform and educational and economic opportunity rang hollow. Four decades had passed since the Nineteenth Amendment granted women the right to vote, yet men continued to dominate politics, the professions, and the business world. While many middle-class white women recognized themselves in Friedan's words, others—younger women, poor women, women of color, lesbians—identified more with the increasingly militant black freedom struggle. More radical feminists concluded that emphasizing rights alone would never revolutionize American gender norms. These women called for liberation in all areas of life.

The women's liberation movement defied a single description. Adopting the slogan "The personal is political," its advocates embraced an expansive meaning of political activism. They confronted patriarchy, racism, homophobia, rape, domestic violence, and workplace discrimination. They challenged cultural norms, such as male ideals of female beauty (Source 27.1) and media representations of women's proper roles (Source 27.4), and produced their own music, literature, and artwork (Source 27.2). They fought for reproductive rights and charged that housework and child care, long devalued as the domain of the housewife, constituted work and deserved recognition as such.

The women's liberation movement faced criticism, and not just from sexist men. Some women, perhaps most famously conservative activist Phyllis Schlafly (Source 27.5), argued that feminists failed to recognize the advantages of being a traditional American woman. Critics cited the supposed benefits of staying home during the day, caring for children, and avoiding the pitfalls of the masculine world, such as work stress and the military draft. Women's liberation activists also argued among themselves. Some radical feminists claimed that patriarchy was the most significant form of oppression, while socialist feminists and feminists of color argued that sexism was intertwined with capitalism and racism (Source 27.3). These feminists also disagreed about whether men had a place in the struggle for women's liberation. Moreover, many women of color refused to align themselves with the women's liberation movement, insisting that racism and poverty took a far greater toll on their communities than sexism.

The following documents provide examples of the ways in which women fought for and against liberation.

SOURCE 27.1 | *No More Miss America!* (1968)

Perhaps no protest document better reflects the tactics and ideals of the radical feminists than the pamphlet *No More Miss America!* Members of the feminist group New York Radical Women distributed the pamphlet outside the annual pageant in Atlantic City as part of a larger protest against male-sanctioned norms of beauty. This document, the group's ten points of protest, illuminates the members' demands and their rhetoric.

The Ten Points We Protest:

1. *The Degrading Mindless-Boob-Girlie Symbol.* The Pageant contestants epitomize the roles we are all forced to play as women. The parade down the runway blares the metaphor of the 4-H Club county fair, where the nervous animals are judged for teeth, fleece, etc., and where the best "specimen" gets the blue ribbon. So are women in our society forced daily to compete for male approval, enslaved by ludicrous "beauty" standards we ourselves are conditioned to take seriously.

2. *Racism with Roses.* Since its inception in 1921, the Pageant has not had one Black finalist, and this has not been for a lack of test-case contestants. There has never been a Puerto Rican, Alaskan, Hawaiian, or Mexican-American winner. Nor has there ever been a *true* Miss America—an American Indian.

3. *Miss America as Military Death Mascot.* The highlight of her reign each year is a cheerleader-tour of American troops abroad—last year she went to Vietnam to pep-talk our husbands, fathers, sons and boyfriends into dying and killing with a better spirit. She personifies the "unstained patriotic American womanhood our boys are fighting for." The Living Bra and the Dead Soldier. We refuse to be used as Mascots for Murder.

Source: Robin Morgan, ed., *Sisterhood Is Powerful: An Anthology of Writings from the Women's Liberation Movement* (New York: Random House, 1970), 522–24.

4. *The Consumer Con-Game.* Miss America is a walking commercial for the Pageant's sponsors. Wind her up and she plugs your product on promotion tours and TV—all in an "honest, objective" endorsement. What a shill.

5. *Competition Rigged and Unrigged.* We deplore the encouragement of an American myth that oppresses men as well as women: the win-or-you're-worthless competitive disease. The "beauty contest" creates only one winner to be "used" and forty-nine losers who are "useless."

6. *The Woman as Pop Culture Obsolescent Theme.* Spindle, mutilate, and then discard tomorrow. What is so ignored as last year's Miss America? This only reflects the gospel of our society, according to Saint Male: women must be young, juicy, malleable—hence age discrimination and the cult of youth. And we women are brainwashed into believing this ourselves!

7. *The Unbeatable Madonna-Whore Combination.* Miss America and *Playboy's* centerfold are sisters over the skin. To win approval, we must be both sexy and wholesome, delicate but able to cope, demure yet titillatingly bitchy. Deviation of any sort brings, we are told, disaster: "You won't get a man!!"

8. *The Irrelevant Crown on the Throne of Mediocrity.* Miss America represents what women are supposed to be: unoffensive, bland, apolitical. If you are tall, short, over or under what weight The Man prescribes you should be, forget it. Personality, articulateness, intelligence, commitment—unwise. Conformity is the key to the crown—and, by extension, to success in our society.

9. *Miss America as Dream Equivalent To—?* In this reputedly democratic society, where every little boy supposedly can grow up to be President, what can every little girl hope to grow to be? Miss America. That's where it's at. Real power to control our own lives is restricted to men, while women get patronizing pseudo-power, an ermine cloak and a bunch of flowers; men are judged by their actions, women by their appearance.

10. *Miss America as Big Sister Watching You.* The Pageant exercises Thought Control, attempts to sear the Image onto our minds, to further make women oppressed and men oppressors; to enslave us all the more in high-heeled, low-status roles; to inculcate false values in young girls; to use women as beasts of buying; to seduce us to prostitute ourselves before our own oppression.

NO MORE MISS AMERICA!!!

SOURCE 27.2 | Ms. *Magazine Cover* (1972)

In 1972 Gloria Steinem, a founder of NOW, and Dorothy Pittman Hughes, an African American businesswoman and child-care advocate, established *Ms.* The premiere issue of the magazine, which features this cover, appeared in January 1972. The magazine started out as a monthly and now is published quarterly. Steinem explained the motivation behind its creation: "I realized as a journalist that there really was nothing for women to read that was controlled by women, and this caused me along with a number of other women to start *Ms.*"

The Granger Collection, New York

SOURCE 27.3 | NATIONAL BLACK FEMINIST ORGANIZATION, *Statement of Purpose* (1973)

While white and black feminists called for an end to gender discrimination, black women faced unique challenges based on their race and their disproportionate representation among the nation's poor. The National Black Feminist Organization (NBFO) formed in May 1973 at a meeting in the National Organization of Women's offices in New York City. Margaret Stone, a contributing editor at *Ms.* magazine, served as its first chair. The organization's Statement of Purpose detailed its platform. Although the national office of the NBFO folded by the end of the decade, it had 2,000 members at its peak, created a blueprint for future African American feminists, and maintained programs and initiatives in some urban areas like Chicago.

The distorted male-dominated media image of the Women's Liberation Movement has clouded the vital and revolutionary importance of this movement to Third World women, especially black women. The Movement has been characterized as the exclusive property of so-called white middle-class women and any black women seen involved in this Movement have been seen as "selling out," "dividing the race," and an assortment of nonsensical epithets. Black feminists resent these charges and have therefore established The National Black Feminist Organization, in order to address ourselves to the particular and specific needs of the larger, but almost cast-aside half of the black race in Amerikkka, the black woman.

Black women have suffered cruelly in this society from living the phenomenon of being black and female, in a country that is *both* racist and sexist. There has been very little real examination of the damage it has caused on the lives and on the minds of black women. Because we live in a patriarchy, we have allowed a premium to be put on black male suffering. No one of us would minimize the pain or hardship or the cruel and inhumane treatment experienced by the black man. But history, past or present, rarely deals with the malicious abuse put upon the black woman. We were seen as breeders by the master; despised and historically polarized from/by the master's wife; and looked upon as castrators by our lovers and husbands. The black woman has had to be strong, yet we are persecuted for having survived. We have been called "matriarchs" by white racists and black nationalists; we have virtually no positive self-images to validate our existence. Black women want to be proud, dignified, and free from all those false definitions of beauty and womanhood that are unrealistic and unnatural. *We,* not white men or black men, must define our own self-image as black women and not fall into the mistake of being placed upon the pedestal which is even being rejected by white women. It has been hard for black women to emerge from the myriad of distorted images that have portrayed us as grinning Beulahs, castrating Sapphires, and pancake-box Jemimas. As black feminists we realized the need to establish ourselves as an independent black feminist organization. Our aboveground presence will lend enormous credibility to the current Women's

Source: Miriam Schneir, ed., *Feminists in Our Time: The Essential Writings, World War II to the Present* (New York: Vintage Books, 1974), 173–74.

Liberation Movement, which unfortunately is not seen as the serious political and economic revolutionary force that it is. We will strengthen the current efforts of the Black Liberation struggle in this country by encouraging *all* of the talents and creativities of black women to emerge, strong and beautiful, not to feel guilty or divisive, and assume positions of leadership and honor in the black community. We will encourage the black community to stop falling into the trap of the white male Left, utilizing women only in terms of domestic or servile needs. We will continue to remind the Black Liberation Movement that there can't be liberation for half the race. We must, together, as a people, work to eliminate racism, from without the black community, which is trying to destroy us as an entire people; but we must remember that sexism is destroying and crippling us from within.

SOURCE 27.4 | PAT MAINARDI, *The Politics of Housework* (1970)

Author Pat Mainardi, who was a member of the radical feminist Redstockings group, recognized that the politics of gender went beyond the voting booth or the workplace. Patriarchy influenced every aspect of society, perhaps none more so than the home. In the following excerpt, Mainardi satirizes her husband's evasive responses to the idea that he share the burden of housework. "The Politics of Housework" reveals that work inside the home held as much relevance for advocates of women's liberation as work outside it.

On the other hand is women's liberation—and housework. What? You say this is all trivial? Wonderful! That's what I thought. It seemed perfectly reasonable. We both had careers, both had to work a couple of days a week to earn enough to live on, so why shouldn't we share the housework? So I suggested it to my mate and he agreed—most men are too hip to turn you down flat. "You're right," he said, "It's only fair."

Then an interesting thing happened. I can only explain it by stating that we women have been brainwashed more than even we can imagine. Probably too many years of seeing television women in ecstasy over their shiny waxed floors or breaking down over their dirty shirt collars. Men have no such conditioning. They recognize the essential fact of housework right from the very beginning. Which is that it stinks. . . . The longer my husband contemplated these chores, the more repulsed he became, and so proceeded the change from the normally sweet considerate Dr. Jekyll into the crafty Mr. Hyde who would stop at nothing to avoid the horrors of—*housework*. As he felt himself backed into a corner laden with dirty dishes, brooms, mops, and reeking garbage, his front teeth grew longer and pointier, his fingernails haggled and his eyes grew wild. Housework trivial? Not on your life! Just try to share the burden.

So ensued a dialogue that's been going on for several years. Here are some of the high points:

Source: Robin Morgan, ed., *Sisterhood Is Powerful: An Anthology of Writings from the Women's Liberation Movement* (New York: Random House, 1970), 447–51.

"I don't mind sharing the housework, but I don't do it very well. We should each do the things we're best at."

Meaning: Unfortunately I'm no good at things like washing dishes or cooking. What I do best is a little light carpentry, changing light bulbs, moving furniture (*how often do you move furniture?*).

Also Meaning: Historically the lower classes (black men and us) have had hundreds of years experience doing menial jobs. It would be a waste of manpower to train someone else to do them now.

Also Meaning: I don't like the dull stupid boring jobs, so you should do them.

"I don't mind sharing the work, but you'll have to show me how to do it."

Meaning: I ask a lot of questions and you'll have to show me everything every time I do it because I don't remember so good. Also don't try to sit down and read while I'm doing my jobs because I'm going to annoy the hell out of you until it's easier to do them yourself.

"We used to be so happy!" (Said whenever it was his turn to do something.)

Meaning: I used to be so happy.

Meaning: Life without housework is bliss. (*No quarrel here. Perfect agreement.*) . . .

"I *hate* it more than you. You don't mind it so much."

Meaning: Housework is garbage work. It's the worst crap I've ever done. It's degrading and humiliating for someone of *my* intelligence to do it. But for someone of *your* intelligence . . .

"Housework is too trivial to even talk about."

Meaning: It's even more trivial to do. Housework is beneath my status. My purpose in life is to deal with matters of significance. Yours is to deal with matters of insignificance. You should do the housework.

"This problem of housework is not a man-woman problem! In any relationship between two people one is going to have a stronger personality and dominate."

Meaning: That stronger personality had better be *me*.

"In animal societies, wolves, for example, the top animal is usually a male even where he is not chosen for brute strength but on the basis of cunning and intelligence. Isn't that interesting?"

Meaning: I have historical, psychological, anthropological, and biological justification for keeping you down. How can you ask the top wolf to be equal?

"Women's liberation isn't really a political movement."

Meaning: The Revolution is coming too close to home.

Also Meaning: I am only interested in how *I* am oppressed, not how I oppress others. Therefore the war, the draft, and the university are political. Women's liberation is not.

"Man's accomplishments have always depended on getting help from other people, mostly women. What great man would have accomplished what he did if he had to do his own housework?"

Meaning: Oppression is built into the System and I, as the white American male, receive the benefits of this System. I don't want to give them up.

SOURCE 27.5 | PHYLLIS SCHLAFLY, *What's Wrong with "Equal Rights" for Women?* (1972)

Phyllis Schlafly, a white mother of six, emerged as the foremost critic of the women's liberation movement in the 1970s. Schlafly believed that feminists foolishly abdicated their responsibilities as women. She began the "Stop ERA" campaign in 1972, which, combined with her 1977 book, *The Power of the Positive Woman*, rallied women to oppose the Equal Rights Amendment, a constitutional amendment that was then being considered by the states for ratification. Schlafly herself worked outside the home as a successful lawyer in St. Louis. The following document is an excerpt from her 1972 essay, "What's Wrong with 'Equal Rights' for Women?"

Of all the classes of people who ever lived, the American woman is the most privileged. We have the most rights and rewards, and the fewest duties. Our unique status is the result of a fortunate combination of circumstances.

1. We have the immense good fortune to live in a civilization which respects the family as the basic unit of society. This respect is part and parcel of our laws and our customs. It is based on the fact of life — which no legislation or agitation can erase — that women have babies and men don't.

   If you don't like this fundamental difference, you will have to take up your complaint with God because He created us this way. The fact that women, not men, have babies is not the fault of selfish and domineering men, or of the establishment, or of any clique of conspirators who want to oppress women. It's simply the way God made us. . . .

The Financial Benefits of Chivalry

2. The second reason why American women are a privileged group is that we are the beneficiaries of a tradition of special respect for women which dates from the Christian Age of Chivalry. The honor and respect paid to Mary, the Mother of Christ, resulted in all women, in effect, being put on a pedestal. . . .

Source: Donald T. Critchlow and Nancy McLean, eds., *Debating the American Conservative Movement, 1945 to the Present* (New York: Rowman and Littlefield, 2009), 197–99.

In other civilizations, such as the African and the American Indian, the men strut around wearing feathers and beads and hunting and fishing (great sport for men!), while the women do all the hard, tiresome drudgery including the tilling of the soil (if any is done), the hewing of wood, the making of fires, the carrying of water, as well as the cooking, sewing and caring for babies.

This is not the American way because we were lucky enough to inherit the traditions of the Age of Chivalry. In America, a man's first significant purchase is a diamond for his bride, and the largest financial investment of his life is a home for her to live in. American husbands work hours of overtime to buy a fur piece or other finery to keep their wives in fashion, and to pay premiums on their life insurance policies to provide for her comfort when she is a widow (benefits in which he can never share).

The Real Liberation of Women

3. The third reason why American women are so well off is that the great American free enterprise system has produced remarkable inventors who have lifted the backbreaking "women's work" from our shoulders. . . .

   The real liberation of women from the backbreaking drudgery of centuries is the American free enterprise system which stimulated inventive geniuses to pursue their talents—and we all reap the profits. The great heroes of women's liberation are not the straggly-haired women on television talk shows and picket lines, but Thomas Edison who brought the miracle of electricity to our homes to give light and to run all those labor-saving devices—the equivalent, perhaps, of a half-dozen household servants for every middle-class American woman. Or Elias Howe who gave us the sewing machine which resulted in such an abundance of readymade clothing. Or Clarence Birdseye who invented the process for freezing foods. Or Henry Ford, who mass-produced the automobile so that it is within the price-range of every American, man or woman.

INTERPRET THE EVIDENCE

1. According to New York Radical Women, how had male ideas of "what women are supposed to be" constrained women's lives (Source 27.1)? What range of issues did these radical feminists raise?

2. Analyze the specific concerns represented on the cover of *Ms.* (Source 27.2). Describe the audience at which the magazine is aimed and evaluate the effectiveness of the cover image.

3. According to the National Black Feminist Organization, what were the unique problems black women faced (Source 27.3)? How did they see their relationship to white feminists and to the male-dominated black liberation movement?

4. In what ways did Pat Mainardi and Phyllis Schlafly disagree over the nature of housework (Sources 27.4 and 27.5)? How does Mainardi's focus on housework fit

with the demands of New York Radical Women and the National Black Feminist Organization?

5. What was Phyllis Schlafly's definition of women's liberation (Source 27.5)? Who do you think might have agreed with her analysis? Who, aside from radical feminists, might have disagreed?

PUT IT IN CONTEXT

1. Where do the agendas of the various advocates of women's liberation overlap, and where do they differ?

2. How does feminism compare with the other progressive social movements of the 1960s and 1970s?

Ronald Reagan and the End of the Cold War

▶ Evaluate the role played by President Reagan in comparison to that played by others in bringing the Cold War to an end.

Ronald Reagan's election to the presidency in 1980 led to an escalation of tensions with the Soviet Union. Reagan wanted to do more than "contain" communism, the foreign policy approach of every American president since Truman, and pursued aggressive defense spending to challenge the Soviets with both conventional and nuclear arms buildups (Source 28.1). One of his programs, the Strategic Defense Initiative (SDI), became particularly controversial. In theory, SDI would have created an antiballistic missile shield over the United States, making it invulnerable to nuclear weapons strikes. Dubbed "Star Wars" for its fanciful theory, which most experts believed to be more fiction than science, the program was also plagued by exorbitant costs and the charge that it violated existing nuclear arms treaties (Source 28.3).

While many in the United States applauded Reagan's tough posture toward the Soviets, he also faced his share of critics (Source 28.2). His military spending combined with lower taxes to create a massive federal deficit. Reagan's use of exaggerated Cold War rhetoric increased anxieties of nuclear confrontation throughout the world. In the long run, however, Reagan was more flexible than his rhetoric implied, and he eventually pursued peaceful coexistence with the Soviets (Source 28.4). By the end of his two terms in office, Reagan had signed treaties with the Soviets to curtail the risk of nuclear war. In decreasing tensions, however, he must share credit with Mikhail Gorbachev, who, in seeking to restructure the Soviet Union along the lines of economic and political openness, embraced cooperation with the United States (Source 28.5).

The following documents examine the Reagan administration as it sought to fight the Cold War and then bring it to an end.

SOURCE 28.1 | RONALD REAGAN, *Remarks at the Annual Convention of the National Association of Evangelicals* (1983)

In the following address before the annual convention of the National Association of Evangelicals, Ronald Reagan revealed his thoughts on a number of subjects related to the relationship between religion and government, morality and society, and the need to defeat what he called the "evil empire" of the Soviet Union. He strongly opposed the nuclear freeze movement, which activists like Barbara Deming and the Women's Peace Encampment supported.

Well, I'm pleased to be here today with you who are keeping America great by keeping her good. Only through your work and prayers and those of millions of others can we hope to survive this perilous century and keep alive this experiment in liberty, this last, best hope of man.

I want you to know that this administration is motivated by a political philosophy that sees the greatness of America in you, her people, and in your families, churches, neighborhoods, communities—the institutions that foster and nourish values like concern for others and respect for the rule of law under God.

Now, I don't have to tell you that this puts us in opposition to, or at least out of step with, a prevailing attitude of many who have turned to a modern-day secularism, discarding the tried and time-tested values upon which our very civilization is based. No matter how well intentioned, their value system is radically different from that of most Americans. And while they proclaim that they're freeing us from superstitions of the past, they've taken upon themselves the job of superintending us by government rule and regulation. Sometimes their voices are louder than ours, but they are not yet a majority. . . .

During my first press conference as President, in answer to a direct question, I pointed out that, as good Marxist-Leninists, the Soviet leaders have openly and publicly declared that the only morality they recognize is that which will further their cause, which is world revolution. I think I should point out I was only quoting Lenin, their guiding spirit, who said in 1920 that they repudiate all morality that proceeds from supernatural ideas—that's their name for religion—or ideas that are outside class conceptions. Morality is entirely subordinate to the interests of class war. And everything is moral that is necessary for the annihilation of the old, exploiting social order and for uniting the proletariat.

Well, I think the refusal of many influential people to accept this elementary fact of Soviet doctrine illustrates an historical reluctance to see totalitarian powers for what they are. We saw this phenomenon in the 1930s. We see it too often today.

This doesn't mean we should isolate ourselves and refuse to seek an understanding with them. I intend to do everything I can to persuade them of our peaceful intent, to remind them that it was the West that refused to use its nuclear

---

Source: "Remarks at the Annual Convention of the National Association of Evangelicals, March 8, 1983," The Ronald Reagan Presidential Foundation, http://www.reaganfoundation.org.

monopoly in the forties and fifties for territorial gain and which now proposes a 50-percent cut in strategic ballistic missiles and the elimination of an entire class of land-based, intermediate-range nuclear missiles.

At the same time, however, they must be made to understand we will never compromise our principles and standards. We will never give away our freedom. We will never abandon our belief in God. And we will never stop searching for a genuine peace. But we can assure none of these things America stands for through the so-called nuclear freeze solutions proposed by some.

The truth is that a freeze now would be a very dangerous fraud, for that is merely the illusion of peace. The reality is that we must find peace through strength.

I would agree to a freeze if only we could freeze the Soviets' global desires. A freeze at current levels of weapons would remove any incentive for the Soviets to negotiate seriously in Geneva and virtually end our chances to achieve the major arms reductions which we have proposed. Instead, they would achieve their objectives through the freeze.

A freeze would reward the Soviet Union for its enormous and unparalleled military buildup. It would prevent the essential and long overdue modernization of United States and allied defenses and would leave our aging forces increasingly vulnerable. And an honest freeze would require extensive prior negotiations on the systems and numbers to be limited and on the measures to ensure effective verification and compliance. And the kind of a freeze that has been suggested would be virtually impossible to verify. Such a major effort would divert us completely from our current negotiations on achieving substantial reductions. . . .

Yes, let us pray for the salvation of all of those who live in that totalitarian darkness—pray they will discover the joy of knowing God. But until they do, let us be aware that while they preach the supremacy of the state, declare its omnipotence over individual man, and predict its eventual domination of all peoples on the Earth, they are the focus of evil in the modern world.

It was C. S. Lewis who, in his unforgettable "Screwtape Letters," wrote: "The greatest evil is not done now in those sordid 'dens of crime' that Dickens loved to paint. It is not even done in concentration camps and labor camps. In those we see its final result. But it is conceived and ordered (moved, seconded, carried and minuted) in clear, carpeted, warmed, and well-lighted offices, by quiet men with white collars and cut fingernails and smooth-shaven cheeks who do not need to raise their voice."

Well, because these "quiet men" do not "raise their voices," because they sometimes speak in soothing tones of brotherhood and peace, because, like other dictators before them, they're always making "their final territorial demand," some would have us accept them at their word and accommodate ourselves to their aggressive impulses. But if history teaches anything, it teaches that simple-minded appeasement or wishful thinking about our adversaries is folly. It means the betrayal of our past, the squandering of our freedom.

So, I urge you to speak out against those who would place the United States in a position of military and moral inferiority. You know, I've always believed that old Screwtape reserved his best efforts for those of you in the church. So, in your discussions of the nuclear freeze proposals, I urge you to beware the temptation of pride—the temptation of blithely declaring yourselves above it all and label both sides equally at fault, to ignore the facts of history and the aggressive impulses of an evil empire, to simply call the arms race a giant misunderstanding and thereby remove yourself from the struggle between right and wrong and good and evil. . . .

While America's military strength is important, let me add here that I've always maintained that the struggle now going on for the world will never be decided by bombs or rockets, by armies or military might. The real crisis we face today is a spiritual one; at root, it is a test of moral will and faith. . . .

I believe that communism is another sad, bizarre chapter in human history whose last pages even now are being written. I believe this because the source of our strength in the quest for human freedom is not material, but spiritual. And because it knows no limitation, it must terrify and ultimately triumph over those who would enslave their fellow man. For in the words of Isaiah: "He giveth power to the faint; and to them that have no might He increased strength. . . . But they that wait upon the Lord shall renew their strength; they shall mount up with wings as eagles; they shall run, and not be weary."

SOURCE 28.2 | GERALDINE FERRARO, *Vice Presidential Nomination Acceptance Address* (1984)

To challenge the popular Reagan administration in 1984, the Democratic Party nominated Walter F. Mondale for president. Mondale selected New York congresswoman Geraldine Ferraro as his running mate, making her the first woman vice presidential candidate on a major party ticket. In her acceptance speech at the 1984 Democratic National Convention, Ferraro discussed how a Democratic administration would differ from that of the Republicans.

Let no one doubt, we will defend America's security and the cause of freedom around the world. But we want a President who tells us what America's fighting for, not just what we are fighting against.

We want a President who will defend human rights, not just where it is convenient, but wherever freedom is at risk—from Chile to Afghanistan, from Poland to South Africa. To those who have watched this administration's confusion in the Middle East, as it has tilted first toward one and then another of Israel's long-time enemies and wonder: "Will America stand by her friends and sister democracy?" we say: America knows who her friends are in the Middle East and around the world. America will stand with Israel always.

Finally, we want a President who will keep America strong, but use that strength to keep America and the world at peace. A nuclear freeze is not a slogan: It is a tool for survival in the nuclear age. If we leave our children nothing else, let us leave them this Earth as we found it: whole and green and full of life.

Source: Geraldine Ferraro, Vice Presidential Nomination Acceptance Address, July 19, 1984.

SOURCE 28.3 | TONY AUTH, *Cartoon*, Philadelphia Inquirer (c. 1988)

Reagan's Strategic Defense Initiative was widely lampooned as too fantastical to be implemented. It was often compared with popular science fiction of the day, as is seen in the following cartoon by Tony Auth.

SOURCE 28.4 | RONALD REAGAN, *Address at Moscow State University* (1988)

By the end of his second term, President Reagan had reduced tensions with the Soviet Union, a nation that just five years earlier he had labeled an "evil empire." He was able to do this partly through a massive military buildup in the United States but also because of the leadership of the new Soviet leader Mikhail Gorbachev, a reformer who brought economic and political changes to the Soviet Union. After fighting a costly and increasingly unpopular decade-long war in Afghanistan, the Soviets did not want to continue an expensive arms race. Reagan was invited to the Soviet Union by Gorbachev for an arms control summit in 1988, where he spoke to university students in Moscow and outlined his hope for greater cooperation between the Cold War adversaries.

As you know, I've come to Moscow to meet with one of your most distinguished graduates. In this, our fourth summit, General Secretary Gorbachev and I have spent many hours together, and I feel that we're getting to know each other well. Our discussions, of course, have been focused primarily on many of the important issues of the day, issues I want to touch on with you in a few moments. But first I want to take a little time to talk to you much as I would to any group of university students in the United States. I want to talk not just of the realities of today but of the possibilities of tomorrow.

Standing here before a mural of your revolution, I want to talk about a very different revolution that is taking place right now, quietly sweeping the globe without bloodshed or conflict. Its effects are peaceful, but they will fundamentally alter our world, shatter old assumptions, and reshape our lives. It's easy to underestimate because it's not accompanied by banners or fanfare. It's been called the technological or information revolution, and as its emblem, one might take the tiny silicon chip, no bigger than a fingerprint. One of these chips has more computing power than a roomful of old-style computers.

As part of an exchange program, we now have an exhibition touring your country that shows how information technology is transforming our lives—replacing manual labor with robots, forecasting weather for farmers, or mapping the genetic code of DNA for medical researchers. These microcomputers today aid the design of everything from houses to cars to spacecraft; they even design better and faster computers. They can translate English into Russian or enable the blind to read or help Michael Jackson produce on one synthesizer the sounds of a whole orchestra. Linked by a network of satellites and fiber-optic cables, one individual with a desktop computer and a telephone commands resources unavailable to the largest governments just a few years ago. . . .

But progress is not foreordained. The key is freedom—freedom of thought, freedom of information, freedom of communication. The renowned scientist, scholar, and founding father of this university, Mikhail Lomonosov, knew that. "It is common knowledge," he said, "that the achievements of science are considerable

Source: Ronald Reagan, "Address at Moscow State University, May 31, 1988," Miller Center, University of Virginia, http://millercenter.org/scripps/archive/speeches/detail/3416.

and rapid, particularly once the yoke of slavery is cast off and replaced by the freedom of philosophy." You know, one of the first contacts between your country and mine took place between Russian and American explorers. The Americans were members of Cook's last voyage on an expedition searching for an Arctic passage; on the island of Unalaska, they came upon the Russians, who took them in, and together with the native inhabitants, held a prayer service on the ice. . . .

We Americans make no secret of our belief in freedom. In fact, it's something of a national pastime. Every four years the American people choose a new President, and 1988 is one of those years. At one point there were 13 major candidates running in the two major parties, not to mention all the others, including the Socialist and Libertarian candidates—all trying to get my job. About 1,000 local television stations, 8,500 radio stations, and 1,700 daily newspapers—each one an independent, private enterprise, fiercely independent of the Government—report on the candidates, grill them in interviews, and bring them together for debates. In the end, the people vote; they decide who will be the next President. But freedom doesn't begin or end with elections.

Go to any American town, to take just an example, and you'll see dozens of churches, representing many different beliefs—in many places, synagogues and mosques—and you'll see families of every conceivable nationality worshiping together. Go into any schoolroom, and there you will see children being taught the Declaration of Independence, that they are endowed by their Creator with certain unalienable rights—among them life, liberty, and the pursuit of happiness—that no government can justly deny; the guarantees in their Constitution for freedom of speech, freedom of assembly, and freedom of religion. Go into any courtroom, and there will preside an independent judge, beholden to no government power. There every defendant has the right to a trial by a jury of his peers, usually 12 men and women—common citizens; they are the ones, the only ones, who weigh the evidence and decide on guilt or innocence. In that court, the accused is innocent until proven guilty, and the word of a policeman or any official has no greater legal standing than the word of the accused. Go to any university campus, and there you'll find an open, sometimes heated discussion of the problems in American society and what can be done to correct them. . . .

But freedom is more even than this. Freedom is the right to question and change the established way of doing things. It is the continuing revolution of the marketplace. It is the understanding that allows us to recognize shortcomings and seek solutions. It is the right to put forth an idea, scoffed at by the experts, and watch it catch fire among the people. It is the right to dream—to follow your dream or stick to your conscience, even if you're the only one in a sea of doubters. Freedom is the recognition that no single person, no single authority or government has a monopoly on the truth, but that every individual life is infinitely precious, that every one of us put on this world has been put there for a reason and has something to offer. . . .

But I hope you know I go on about these things not simply to extol the virtues of my own country but to speak to the true greatness of the heart and soul of your land. Who, after all, needs to tell the land of Dostoyevsky about the quest for truth, the home of Kandinsky and Scriabin about imagination, the rich and noble culture of the Uzbek man of letters Alisher Navoi about beauty and heart? The great culture of your diverse land speaks with a glowing passion to all humanity. Let me cite one of the most eloquent contemporary passages on human freedom. It comes, not from the literature of America, but from this country, from one of the greatest writers of the 20th century, Boris Pasternak, in the novel *Dr. Zhivago*. He writes: "I think that if the beast who sleeps in man could be held down by threats—any kind of threat, whether of jail or of retribution after death—then the highest emblem of humanity would be the lion tamer in the circus with his whip, not the prophet who sacrificed himself. But this is just the point—what has for centuries raised man above the beast is not the cudgel, but an inward music—the irresistible power of unarmed truth." . . .

Just a few years ago, few would have imagined the progress our two nations have made together. The INF treaty, which General Secretary Gorbachev and I signed last December in Washington and whose instruments of ratification we will exchange tomorrow—the first true nuclear arms reduction treaty in history, calling for the elimination of an entire class of U.S. and Soviet nuclear missiles. And just 16 days ago, we saw the beginning of your withdrawal from Afghanistan, which gives us hope that soon the fighting may end and the healing may begin and that that suffering country may find self-determination, unity, and peace at long last. . . .

We do not know what the conclusion will be of this journey, but we're hopeful that the promise of reform will be fulfilled. In this Moscow spring, this May 1988, we may be allowed that hope: that freedom, like the fresh green sapling planted over Tolstoy's grave, will blossom forth at last in the rich fertile soil of your people and culture. We may be allowed to hope that the marvelous sound of a new openness will keep rising through, ringing through, leading to a new world of reconciliation, friendship, and peace.

Thank you all very much, and *da blagoslovit vas gospod*—God bless you.

SOURCE 28.5 | MIKHAIL GORBACHEV, *Speech before the Central Committee* (January 27, 1987)

In 1985 Mikhail Gorbachev became the new leader of the Soviet Union. The first leader born after the Russian Revolution, Gorbachev sought to strengthen communism by reforming it. His policy of *perestroika* was meant to restructure the flagging Soviet command economy, while *glasnost* gave Soviet citizens new political freedoms. In 1987 he outlined the reasons for these changes to the Soviet Central Committee, excerpted here.

Source: From "End of the Cold War," *Everyday Americans, Exceptional Americans: A Teaching American History Project*, http://chnm.gmu.edu/tah-loudoun/blog/psas/end-of-the-cold-war/.

Comrades,

The 27th Party Congress vested in us, the members of the Central Committee, an immense responsibility—to implement the strategic course of accelerating the socio-economic development of the country. . . .

   The main evaluations of the state of society and the conclusions drawn from them by the Political Bureau have already been presented to the 27th Party Congress and Plenary Meetings of the Central Committee. They have been fully corroborated. But today we know more, that is why there is a need to examine once again and in detail the sources of the obtaining situation and to sort out the reasons for what took place in the country in the late 1970s and early 1980s.

   This analysis is necessary to prevent mistakes from recurring and to fulfill the resolutions of the Congress on which the future of our people and the destiny of socialism depend. It is all the more important since there is still some mis-understanding in society and in the Party of the complexity of the situation in which the country has found itself. Perhaps, this also explains questions from some comrades about the measures that are being taken by the Political Bureau and the government in the course of reorganization. We are often asked if we are not taking too sharp a turn. . . .

   Our achievements are immense and indubitable and the Soviet people by right take pride in their successes. They constitute a firm base for the fulfillment of our current programs and our plans for the future. But the Party must see life in its entirety and complexity. No accomplishments, even the most impressive ones, should obscure either contradictions in social development or our mistakes and failings. . . .

   Of course, Comrades, the country did not cease to develop. Tens of millions of Soviet people were working honestly and many Party organizations and our personnel were working actively in the interests of the people. All that held back the intensification of negative processes but could not avert them altogether.

   A need for change was ripening in the economy and other fields—but it did not materialize in the political and practical work of the Party and the state. What was the reason for that complex and controversial situation?

   The main cause—and the Political Bureau considers it necessary to say so with utmost frankness at the Plenary Meeting—was that the CPSU Central Committee and the leadership of the country failed, primarily for subjective rea-sons, to see in time and in full the need for change and the dangerous growth of crisis phenomena in society, and to formulate a clear-cut policy for overcoming them and making better use of the possibilities intrinsic to the socialist system. . . .

   Reorganization is a resolute overcoming of the processes of stagnation, destruction of the retarding mechanism, and the creation of dependable and effi-cient machinery for expediting the social and economic progress of Soviet society. The main purport of our strategy is to combine the achievements of the scientific and technological revolution with a plan-based economy and set the entire poten-tial of socialism in motion. . . .

The final aim of reorganization is, I believe, clear: it is to effect thorough-going changes in all aspects of public life, to give socialism the most advanced form of social organization, and bring out to the utmost the humane nature of our system in all decisive aspects—economic, social, political and moral. . . .

It is only through the consistent development of the democratic forms inherent in socialism and more extensive self-government that our progress in production, science and technology, literature, culture and the arts, in all areas of social life is possible. It is only this way that ensures conscientious discipline. The reorganization itself is possible only through democracy and due to democracy. It is only this way that it is possible to open broad vistas for socialism's most powerful creative force—free labour and free thought in a free country. . . .

Comrades, there isn't one single fundamental issue that we could resolve, now as in the past, without taking into account the fact that we live in a multi-national country. There is no need to prove the importance of socialist principles in the development of relations between the nationalities. It is socialism that did away with national oppression, inequality, and infringements upon the rights of people on grounds of nationality. It ensured the economic and cultural progress of all nationalities and ethnic groups. In short, the successes of our Party's nationalities policy are beyond any doubt and we can justly take pride in them. . . .

INTERPRET THE EVIDENCE

1. How does President Ronald Reagan describe the relationship between the United States and the Soviet Union in the early 1980s (Sources 28.1 and 28.4)? What connections does he make between religion and foreign policy?

2. What does Geraldine Ferraro say is wrong with the foreign policy of Ronald Reagan (Source 28.2)? According to Ferraro, how would a Democratic administration do things differently?

3. In what ways is Tony Auth's cartoon making fun of the science behind SDI (Source 28.3)? What does Auth argue about SDI's effect on Reagan?

4. In his speech to students at Moscow State University, how does President Reagan define "freedom" (Source 28.4)? How does he use Russian history to gain support for his message? What does he say has changed since his "evil empire" speech?

5. What evidence does Mikhail Gorbachev use to defend his reform policies (Source 28.5)? What is he hoping to achieve with these new policies? What does Gorbachev mean by "democracy" and "freedom"?

PUT IT IN CONTEXT

1. What role did the Reagan administration play in ending the Cold War? What circumstances made the cessation of hostilities feasible?

The Environment and Federal Policy in the Twenty-First Century

▶ Analyze the factors that have brought environmental concerns to the forefront of American politics during the last several decades.

Debates over environmental issues accelerated at the start of the twenty-first century. The federal government has struggled to articulate a coherent environmental policy, even as politicians, scholars, activists, and writers have all recognized that increasing globalization and scientific evidence of climate change have made environmental questions much more urgent (Source 29.2). At the highest level, Presidents George W. Bush (Source 29.1), Barack Obama (Source 29.3), and Donald Trump (Source 29.4) examined the ways in which the environment and the economy are interwoven (although they came to different conclusions). During their presidencies, the United States experienced three catastrophic events—Hurricane Katrina in 2005, the BP oil spill in 2010, and Hurricanes Harvey, Irma, and Maria (Source 29.5) in 2017—that led to additional questions about the government's preparedness to deal with environmental problems. The powerful hurricanes demonstrated that environmental distress disproportionately affects poor and minority populations. Global warming, oil prices, and alternative energy have all become major political flash points.

The following sources shed light on these ongoing debates concerning the government and the environment. Like most issues presented in the final chapter of the book, federal environmental policy remains in flux.

SOURCE 29.1 | GEORGE W. BUSH, *Press Release on Global Climate Change* (2001)

In 1997 the United States and fifty-four other nations pledged to reduce greenhouse gas emissions in the Kyoto treaty. But before the treaty could become binding in 2005, George

Source: "President Bush Discusses Global Climate Change, June 11, 2001," White House Archives, http://georgewbush-whitehouse.archives.gov/news/releases/2001/06/20010611-2.html.

W. Bush announced that the nation would not agree to the Kyoto protocol. In the following address, released June 11, 2001, the new president discussed his reasons for not ratifying the treaty.

There is a natural greenhouse effect that contributes to warming. Greenhouse gases trap heat, and thus warm the earth because they prevent a significant proportion of infrared radiation from escaping into space. Concentration of greenhouse gases, especially CO_2, have increased substantially since the beginning of the industrial revolution. And the National Academy of Sciences indicate[s] that the increase is due in large part to human activity.

Yet, the Academy's report tells us that we do not know how much effect natural fluctuations in climate may have had on warming. We do not know how much our climate could, or will, change in the future. We do not know how fast change will occur, or even how some of our actions could impact it.

For example, our useful efforts to reduce sulfur emissions may have actually increased warming, because sulfate particles reflect sunlight, bouncing it back into space. And, finally, no one can say with any certainty what constitutes a dangerous level of warming, and therefore what level must be avoided.

The policy challenge is to act in a serious and sensible way, given the limits of our knowledge. . . .

Our country, the United States, is the world's largest emitter of man-made greenhouse gases. We account for almost 20 percent of the world's man-made greenhouse emissions. We also account for about one-quarter of the world's economic output. We recognize the responsibility to reduce our emissions. We also recognize the other part of the story — that the rest of the world emits 80 percent of all greenhouse gases. And many of those emissions come from developing countries.

This is a challenge that requires a 100 percent effort; ours, and the rest of the world's. The world's second-largest emitter of greenhouse gases is China. Yet, China was entirely exempted from the requirements of the Kyoto Protocol.

India and Germany are among the top emitters. Yet, India was also exempt from Kyoto. These and other developing countries that are experiencing rapid growth face challenges in reducing their emissions without harming their economies. We want to work cooperatively with these countries in their efforts to reduce greenhouse emissions and maintain economic growth.

Kyoto also failed to address two major pollutants that have an impact on warming: black soot and tropospheric ozone. Both are proven health hazards. Reducing both would not only address climate change, but also dramatically improve people's health.

Kyoto is, in many ways, unrealistic. Many countries cannot meet their Kyoto targets. The targets themselves were arbitrary and not based upon science. For America, complying with those mandates would have a negative economic impact, with layoffs of workers and price increases for consumers. And when you evaluate all these flaws, most reasonable people will understand that it's not sound public policy.

That's why 95 members of the United States Senate expressed a reluctance to endorse such an approach. Yet, America's unwillingness to embrace a flawed treaty should not be read by our friends and allies as any abdication of responsibility. To the contrary, my administration is committed to a leadership role on the issue of climate change.

We recognize our responsibility and will meet it—at home, in our hemisphere, and in the world. My Cabinet-level working group on climate change is recommending a number of initial steps, and will continue to work on additional ideas. The working group proposes the United States help lead the way by advancing the science on climate change, advancing the technology to monitor and reduce greenhouse gases, and creating partnerships within our hemisphere and beyond to monitor and measure and mitigate emissions. . . .

By increasing conservation and energy efficiency and aggressively using these clean energy technologies, we can reduce our greenhouse gas emissions by significant amounts in the coming years. We can make great progress in reducing emissions, and we will. Yet, even that isn't enough.

I've asked my advisors to consider approaches to reduce greenhouse gas emissions, including those that tap the power of markets, help realize the promise of technology and ensure the widest-possible global participation. As we analyze the possibilities, we will be guided by several basic principles. Our approach must be consistent with the long-term goal of stabilizing greenhouse gas concentrations in the atmosphere. Our actions should be measured as we learn more from science and build on it.

Our approach must be flexible to adjust to new information and take advantage of new technology. We must always act to ensure continued economic growth and prosperity for our citizens and for citizens throughout the world. We should pursue market-based incentives and spur technological innovation.

And, finally, our approach must be based on global participation, including that of developing countries whose net greenhouse gas emissions now exceed those in the developed countries.

SOURCE 29.2 | LESTER BROWN, *Outgrowing the Earth* (2004)

Lester Brown, the founder of the Worldwatch Institute and a former member of the U.S. Department of Agriculture's Foreign Agricultural Service, has for decades been one of the nation's leading environmentalists. In the following excerpt from his 2004 book, *Outgrowing the Earth*, Brown connects the global environmental crisis with what he calls "food security."

When grain harvests fell short, stocks declined, and prices rose during the last half of the twentieth century, there was a standard response. At the official level, the U.S. government would return to production part or all of the cropland idled under its commodity set-aside programs. At the same time, higher prices would

Source: Lester Brown, *Outgrowing the Earth: The Food Security Challenge in an Age of Falling Water Tables and Rising Temperatures* (New York: W. W. Norton, 2004), 187–92.

encourage farmers worldwide to use more fertilizer, drill more irrigation wells, and invest in other yield-enhancing measures. Production would jump and shortages would disappear.

Now the possible responses to shortages are more demanding. First, the U.S. cropland set-aside program was dismantled in 1996, depriving the world of this longstanding backup reserve for world grain stocks. As of 2004, only the European Union is holding cropland out of use to limit production, but it is a small area, perhaps 3 million hectares. The United States does have some 14 million hectares (35 million acres) of cropland, much of it highly erodible, in the Conservation Reserve Program under 10-year contracts with farmers, nearly all planted in grass. In an emergency, part of it could be plowed and planted in grain, but it is mostly low-rainfall, low-yielding land in the Great Plains that would expand the U.S. harvest only marginally.

The world today faces a situation far different from that of half a century ago. Diminishing returns are setting in on several fronts, including the quality of new land that can be brought under the plow, the production response to additional fertilizer applications, the opportunity for drilling new irrigation wells, and the potential of research investments to produce technologies that will boost production dramatically. . . .

The world has changed in other ways. As world population and the global economy expanded dramatically over the last half-century, the world quietly moved into a new era, one in which the economy began pressing against the earth's natural limits. In this new situation, activities in one economic sector can affect another. Historically, for example, what happened in the transport sector had little effect on agriculture. But in a world with 6.3 billion people, most of whom would like to own a car, auto-centered transport systems will consume a vast area of cropland.

In the societies that first turned to cars as the principal means of transportation, there was no need for the transportation minister to consult with the agriculture minister. During the earlier development of the United States, for example, there was more than enough land for crops and cars. Indeed, throughout much of this era farmers were paid to hold land out of production. Now that has changed. Food security is directly affected by transportation policy today.

If densely populated countries like China and India turn to cars as the primary means of transportation, they will pit affluent automobile owners against low-income food consumers in the competition for land. These nations simply do not have enough land to support hundreds of millions of cars and to feed their people.

The competition between cars and people for resources does not stop here. Some key food-producing countries, including the United States, are producing ethanol from grain for automotive fuel. In 2004, the United States used some 30 million tons of its 278-million-ton corn harvest to manufacture ethanol for cars. This tonnage, requiring nearly 4 million hectares (10 million acres) to produce, would be enough to feed 100 million people at average world consumption levels. Other countries building grain-fed ethanol plants include Canada and China. The competition between affluent motorists and low-income food consumers is thus not only for the land used to produce food, but also for the food itself.

The other side of this coin is that if grain prices rise sharply, ethanol plants are likely to close, as they did in 1996 when grain prices went up temporarily. This would free up grain for food or feed, thus providing an additional buffer when world grain supplies tighten.

The loss of momentum on the food front in recent years argues for reassessing the global population trajectory. Indeed, population policymakers may hold the key to achieving a humane balance between population and food. We can no longer take population projections as a given. The world cannot afford for any women to be without family planning advice and contraceptives. Today, however, an estimated 137 million women want to limit the size of their families but lack access to the family planning services needed to do so. Eradicating hunger depends on filling the family planning gap and creating the social conditions that will accelerate the shift to smaller families.

Food security is affected not only by the food-population equation, but also by the water-population equation and the efforts of water resource ministries to raise water productivity. Indeed, since 70 percent of world water use is for irrigation, eradicating hunger may now depend on a global full-court press to raise water productivity. . . .

Ensuring future food security therefore can no longer be left to ministries of agriculture alone. Food security is now directly dependent on policy decisions in the ministries of health and family planning, water resources, transportation, and energy. This dependence of food security on an integrated effort by several departments of government is new. And because it has emerged so quickly, governments are lagging far behind in their efforts to coordinate these departments and their agendas.

One of the essentials for success in this new situation is strong national political leaders. In the absence of competent leaders who understand the complex interaction of these issues, the cooperation needed to ensure a country's future food security may simply not be forthcoming. In the absence of such leadership, a deterioration in the food situation may be unavoidable.

SOURCE 29.3 | BARACK OBAMA, *State of the Union Address* (2012)

Throughout his 2008 campaign for president, Barack Obama pledged to take a more proactive approach to the environment than George W. Bush. Yet while many environmental activists and scholars have praised his attention to energy efficiency, they have criticized him for promoting Arctic drilling and for not increasing regulations on the oil and natural gas extraction process of hydraulic fracturing, or "fracking." In his January 2012 State of the Union address, Obama discussed his environmental agenda and how it would improve both the climate and the economy.

Source: "Remarks by the President in State of the Union Address, January 24, 2012," The White House, Office of the Press Secretary, http://www.whitehouse.gov/the-press-office/2012/01/24/remarks-president-state-union-address.

And nowhere is the promise of innovation greater than in American-made energy. Over the last three years, we've opened millions of new acres for oil and gas exploration, and tonight, I'm directing my administration to open more than 75 percent of our potential offshore oil and gas resources. Right now—right now—American oil production is the highest that it's been in eight years. That's right—eight years. Not only that—last year, we relied less on foreign oil than in any of the past 16 years.

But with only 2 percent of the world's oil reserves, oil isn't enough. This country needs an all-out, all-of-the-above strategy that develops every available source of American energy. A strategy that's cleaner, cheaper, and full of new jobs.

We have a supply of natural gas that can last America nearly 100 years. And my administration will take every possible action to safely develop this energy. Experts believe this will support more than 600,000 jobs by the end of the decade. And I'm requiring all companies that drill for gas on public lands to disclose the chemicals they use. Because America will develop this resource without putting the health and safety of our citizens at risk.

The development of natural gas will create jobs and power trucks and factories that are cleaner and cheaper, proving that we don't have to choose between our environment and our economy. And by the way, it was public research dollars, over the course of 30 years, that helped develop the technologies to extract all this natural gas out of shale rock—reminding us that government support is critical in helping businesses get new energy ideas off the ground.

Now, what's true for natural gas is just as true for clean energy. In three years, our partnership with the private sector has already positioned America to be the world's leading manufacturer of high-tech batteries. Because of federal investments, renewable energy use has nearly doubled, and thousands of Americans have jobs because of it. . . .

We've subsidized oil companies for a century. That's long enough. It's time to end the taxpayer giveaways to an industry that rarely has been more profitable, and double-down on a clean energy industry that never has been more promising. Pass clean energy tax credits. Create these jobs.

We can also spur energy innovation with new incentives. The differences in this chamber may be too deep right now to pass a comprehensive plan to fight climate change. But there's no reason why Congress shouldn't at least set a clean energy standard that creates a market for innovation. So far, you haven't acted.

Well, tonight, I will. I'm directing my administration to allow the development of clean energy on enough public land to power 3 million homes. And I'm proud to announce that the Department of Defense, working with us, the world's largest consumer of energy, will make one of the largest commitments to clean energy in history—with the Navy purchasing enough capacity to power a quarter of a million homes a year.

Of course, the easiest way to save money is to waste less energy. So here's a proposal: Help manufacturers eliminate energy waste in their factories and give businesses incentives to upgrade their buildings. Their energy bills will be $100 billion lower over the next decade, and America will have less pollution, more manufacturing, more jobs for construction workers who need them. Send me a bill that creates these jobs. . . .

There's no question that some regulations are outdated, unnecessary, or too costly. In fact, I've approved fewer regulations in the first three years of my presidency than my Republican predecessor did in his. I've ordered every federal agency to eliminate rules that don't make sense. We've already announced over 500 reforms, and just a fraction of them will save business and citizens more than $10 billion over the next five years. We got rid of one rule from 40 years ago that could have forced some dairy farmers to spend $10,000 a year proving that they could contain a spill—because milk was somehow classified as an oil. With a rule like that, I guess it was worth crying over spilled milk.

Now, I'm confident a farmer can contain a milk spill without a federal agency looking over his shoulder. Absolutely. But I will not back down from making sure an oil company can contain the kind of oil spill we saw in the Gulf two years ago. I will not back down from protecting our kids from mercury poisoning, or making sure that our food is safe and our water is clean.

SOURCE 29.4 | *Donald Trump Withdraws from the Paris Climate Accord* (June 1, 2017)

Within six months of taking office as president, Donald Trump announced the withdrawal of the United States from the Paris Climate Accord, one of President Obama's signature achievements on global environmental policy. This left the United States as the only one of some 200 nations outside the agreement. In this instance, Trump, who had run on a nationalist, America First platform, fulfilled his campaign pledge to conduct international affairs on behalf of U.S. self-interests. By doing so, he implemented traditional Republican Party policy to diminish federal regulation of business.

. . . As President, I can put no other consideration before the wellbeing of American citizens. The Paris Climate Accord is simply the latest example of Washington entering into an agreement that disadvantages the United States to the exclusive benefit of other countries, leaving American workers—who I love—and taxpayers to absorb the cost in terms of lost jobs, lower wages, shuttered factories, and vastly diminished economic production.

Thus, as of today, the United States will cease all implementation of the non-binding Paris Accord and the draconian financial and economic burdens the agreement imposes on our country. This includes ending the implementation of the nationally determined contribution and, very importantly, the Green Climate Fund which is costing the United States a vast fortune.

Compliance with the terms of the Paris Accord and the onerous energy restrictions it has placed on the United States could cost America as much as 2.7 million lost jobs by 2025 according to the National Economic Research

Source: https://www.whitehouse.gov/briefings-statements/statement-president-trump-paris-climate-accord/

Associates. This includes 440,000 fewer manufacturing jobs—not what we need—believe me, this is not what we need—including automobile jobs, and the further decimation of vital American industries on which countless communities rely. They rely for so much, and we would be giving them so little.

According to this same study, by 2040, compliance with the commitments put into place by the previous administration would cut production for the following sectors: paper down 12 percent; cement down 23 percent; iron and steel down 38 percent; coal—and I happen to love the coal miners—down 86 percent; natural gas down 31 percent. The cost to the economy at this time would be close to $3 trillion in lost GDP and 6.5 million industrial jobs, while households would have $7,000 less income and, in many cases, much worse than that.

Not only does this deal subject our citizens to harsh economic restrictions, it fails to live up to our environmental ideals. As someone who cares deeply about the environment, which I do, I cannot in good conscience support a deal that punishes the United States—which is what it does—the world's leader in environmental protection, while imposing no meaningful obligations on the world's leading polluters.

For example, under the agreement, China will be able to increase these emissions by a staggering number of years—13. They can do whatever they want for 13 years. Not us. India makes its participation contingent on receiving billions and billions and billions of dollars in foreign aid from developed countries. There are many other examples. But the bottom line is that the Paris Accord is very unfair, at the highest level, to the United States.

. . . This agreement is less about the climate and more about other countries gaining a financial advantage over the United States. The rest of the world applauded when we signed the Paris Agreement—they went wild; they were so happy—for the simple reason that it put our country, the United States of America, which we all love, at a very, very big economic disadvantage. A cynic would say the obvious reason for economic competitors and their wish to see us remain in the agreement is so that we continue to suffer this self-inflicted major economic wound. We would find it very hard to compete with other countries from other parts of the world.

We have among the most abundant energy reserves on the planet, sufficient to lift millions of America's poorest workers out of poverty. Yet, under this agreement, we are effectively putting these reserves under lock and key, taking away the great wealth of our nation—it's great wealth, it's phenomenal wealth; not so long ago, we had no idea we had such wealth—and leaving millions and millions of families trapped in poverty and joblessness.

The agreement is a massive redistribution of United States wealth to other countries. At 1 percent growth, renewable sources of energy can meet some of our domestic demand, but at 3 or 4 percent growth, which I expect, we need all forms of available American energy, or our country—(applause)—will be at grave risk of brownouts and blackouts, our businesses will come to a halt in many cases, and the American family will suffer the consequences in the form of lost jobs and a very diminished quality of life.

Even if the Paris Agreement were implemented in full, with total compliance from all nations, it is estimated it would only produce a two-tenths of one degree—think of that; this much—Celsius reduction in global temperature by the year 2100. Tiny, tiny amount. In fact, 14 days of carbon emissions from China alone would wipe out the gains from America—and this is an incredible statistic—would totally wipe out the gains from America's expected reductions in the year 2030, after we have had to spend billions and billions of dollars, lost jobs, closed factories, and suffered much higher energy costs for our businesses and for our homes.

. . . I will work to ensure that America remains the world's leader on environmental issues, but under a framework that is fair and where the burdens and responsibilities are equally shared among the many nations all around the world.

No responsible leader can put the workers—and the people—of their country at this debilitating and tremendous disadvantage. The fact that the Paris deal hamstrings the United States, while empowering some of the world's top polluting countries, should dispel any doubt as to the real reason why foreign lobbyists wish to keep our magnificent country tied up and bound down by this agreement: It's to give their country an economic edge over the United States. That's not going to happen while I'm President. . . .

SOURCE 29.5 | CONNOR MAXWELL AND CATHLEEN KELLY, *Hurricane Maria and the Need for Environmental Justice in Puerto Rico* (2017)

In September 2017, Hurricane Maria struck the U.S. territories of Puerto Rico and the Virgin Islands, causing catastrophic damage to life and property in these Caribbean islands. The official death toll in Puerto Rico was sixty-four, but the actual number may have been in the hundreds. Adding to the human distress, the majority of Puerto Ricans did not recover their electric power for another six months. Although hurricanes are considered natural disasters, the damage they inflict are exacerbated by governmental and corporate decisions. As Connor Maxwell and Cathleen Kelly of the non-profit Center for American Progress show, the damaging effects of Hurricane Maria are rooted in economic and political inequalities stemming from the colonial relationship between the United States and Puerto Rico.

The frequency and severity of extreme weather events such as those seen this year is on the rise as the climate changes. All too often, these events hit low-income communities and communities of color, already overburdened by polluted air and water, the hardest. To help communities in Puerto Rico and other hurricane-affected areas better prepare for the future, Congress should support a comprehensive federal rebuilding package. The package must prioritize areas where people have the fewest resources to rebuild; support an inclusive process

Source: Connor Maxwell and Cathleen Kelly, "3 Million Reasons for Environmental Justice in Puerto Rico," Center for American Progress, October 19, 2017, https://www.americanprogress.org/issues/green/news/2017/10/19/441060/3-million-reasons-environmental-justice-puerto-rico/

to create rebuilding plans; and invest in infrastructure designed to withstand growing extreme weather risks fueled by climate change.

When Hurricane Maria pummeled Puerto Rico with winds whipping at 155 miles per hour, it left in its wake utter catastrophe. The hurricane damaged and destroyed homes and buildings, washed away roadways, and decimated the already shoddy electricity grid, casting the entire island into darkness. Currently, more than 80 percent of the island is still without power and thousands still struggle to find food, shelter, and medical care. People have become so desperate for water that they are even drinking from wells located on extremely hazardous waste sites. The official death toll stands at 48, but some believe the real total will prove much higher—450 or more. . . . As these dire conditions persist, experts have raised concerns about Hurricane Maria's long-term health implications, such as mosquito-borne diseases and life-threatening infections.

In response to their plight, President Donald Trump stated that Puerto Ricans "want everything to be done for them," threatened to abandon the recovery effort, and cast doubt on long-term financial support. . . . Oxfam America, which rarely responds to humanitarian emergencies in the United States, stated, "the US has more than enough resources to mobilize an emergency response but has failed to do so in a swift and robust manner." Retired Lt. Gen. Russel L. Honoré, who led the military response to Hurricane Katrina, noted that the administration was unprepared, sent ships four days too late, and has deployed half as many federal troops, ships, and National Guardsmen as needed. Unfortunately, the administration's sluggish and inadequate hurricane response was predictable and entirely consistent with its 10-month pattern of shortsighted and discriminatory governing.

Earlier this year, President Trump proposed a plan to slash the nation's disaster preparedness and recovery budget by hundreds of billions of dollars. Under his plan, the Federal Emergency Management Agency (FEMA) would lose $667 million in state and local grant funding. He also proposed eliminating the entire $3 billion Community Development Block Grant Program, which, among other things, helps homeowners and businesses in low-income communities rebuild after natural disasters. The administration would also abolish the Environmental Protection Agency (EPA)'s Office of Environmental Justice, which helps low-income communities and communities of color that are overburdened by environmental pollution.

The administration's lethargic response to Hurricanes Maria and Irma has prolonged Puerto Rico's suffering and dangerous living conditions. The United States' history of oppressive colonial and economic policies toward Puerto Rico and its consistent insufficient federal support to the commonwealth are also to blame. Puerto Rico is home to 29 landfills that are overflowing with tons of toxic coal ash and 18 superfund sites—extremely hazardous waste sites identified for long-term cleanup by the EPA. If the storm damaged any of these areas, then contaminants could be seeping into the soil and drinking water of nearby communities, which are typically inhabited by low-income and minority populations.

The commonwealth . . . still faces a declining population and a debt crisis started, in part, by a change in federal tax policy. Even before the storm, nearly half of the island's residents lived in poverty, compared with just 1 in 6 mainland residents, and Puerto Ricans were more than twice as likely to be unemployed. Furthermore, the Army Corps of Engineers rated all 38 dams in Puerto Rico as having a "high hazard potential," but the commonwealth lacks the resources to regularly inspect them on its own. Despite these grave challenges, Puerto Rico receives far less per-capita support in the form of competitive federal grants than states do. Inadequate federal investment in the building blocks of strong communities, such as education, healthcare, housing, environmental protection, and climate resilience, puts American citizens in Puerto Rico at serious risk. But this doesn't have to be the reality.

Like any area hit by a disaster, Puerto Rico needs real leadership from the federal government to help residents pick up the pieces and rebuild their lives. The Trump administration and Congress must provide much-needed support for immediate rescue and relief to alleviate the suffering of millions of American citizens in Puerto Rico.

The administration and Congress must also commit to providing long-term, equitable, and adequate federal assistance to rebuild the island's communities and infrastructure. This includes significant investments to transform Puerto Rico's aging energy infrastructure to eliminate its heavy reliance on imported oil or other fossil fuels, as well as to generate its power using clean, affordable, and reliable renewable energy and storage resources. The federal relief package must also rebuild communities and infrastructure using stronger building codes and designs that withstand the new normal of more extreme weather and sea level rise fueled by climate change. The federal rebuilding package must also prioritize communities with the fewest resources to rebuild and recover from toxic pollution exposure. Finally, the EPA must release the results of its superfund site assessments and immediately launch efforts to clean up and secure any damaged superfund sites to reduce the devastating long-term health impacts for residents. By providing disaster rebuilding assistance that supports safe, strong, and just rebuilding, the federal government can help all U.S. citizens in Puerto Rico recover, while also saving lives and money in the future.

INTERPRET THE EVIDENCE

1. Why did George W. Bush oppose the Kyoto protocol (Source 29.1)? What issues does he prioritize in stating his administration's environmental plans? How does he envision the United States working with the rest of the world to reduce emissions?

2. According to Lester Brown, what new environmental challenges do the United States and the world face (Source 29.2)? How has globalization altered the nature of environmental challenges? How does Brown link the potential for food shortages with national security?

3. How does Barack Obama link the environment to the economy (Source 29.3)? According to Obama, what role should government play in environmental issues? Would George W. Bush disagree with Obama's ideas? Why or why not?

4. Compare Donald Trump's view of the connection between the economy and the environment (Source 29.4) with that of Barack Obama (Source 29.3). In this speech Trump says that he "cares deeply about the environment." What evidence does he provide, if any, in this speech?

5. How does Hurricane Maria (Source 29.5) show that natural disasters are not just "natural"? How would President Trump respond to this analysis (Source 29.4)?

PUT IT IN CONTEXT

1. How is environmental policy connected to other political issues? What factors must government consider when fashioning environmental policy?

Acknowledgments

Source Project 24 24.2 "Document VI: Ciphered Telegram from Shtykov to Vyshinsky, 19 January 1950," *Cold War International History Project Bulletin,* Issue 5 (Washington, D.C.: Woodrow Wilson International Center for Scholars, 1995), 8. Used with permission.

Source Project 25 25.3 Harry Henderson, "The Mass-Produced Suburbs," *Harper's Magazine,* November 1953, 25–32. Copyright © 1953 Harper's Magazine. All rights reserved. Reproduced from the November issue by special permission.

25.4 From the song, "Little Boxes." Words and music by Malvina Reynolds. Copyright © 1962 Schroder Music Co. (ASCAP); Renewed 1990. Used by permission. All rights reserved.

Source Project 27 27.1 "No More Miss America!" from *Sisterhood Is Powerful: An Anthology of Writings from the Women's Liberation Movement,* edited by Robin Morgan, Copyright © 1970 by Robin Morgan (Random House and Vintage Books). All Rights Reserved. Reprinted with permission.

27.3 Miriam Schneir, ed., *FeminISM in Our Time: The Essential Writings, World War II to the Present.* (New York: Vintage Books, 1974), 173–74. Copyright © 1974 by Miriam Schneir. Used with permission.

27.4 Pat Mainardi, "The Politics of Housework," from *Sisterhood Is Powerful: An Anthology of Writings from the Women's Liberation Movement,* edited by Robin Morgan, Copyright © 1970 by Robin Morgan (Random House and Vintage Books). All Rights Reserved. Reprinted with permission.

27.5 Donald T. Critchlow and Nancy McLean, eds., *Debating the American Conservative Movement, 1945 to the Present.* (New York: Rowman and Littlefield, 2009), 197–99. Copyright © 2009 by Rowman and Littlefield. Republished with permission; permission conveyed through Copyright Clearance Center, Inc.

Source Project 29 29.2 Lester Brown, *Outgrowing the Earth: Rising Food Prices, the Growing Politics of Food Scarcity* by Lester Brown. Copyright © 2004 by Earth Policy Institute. Used by permission of W. W. Norton & Company, Inc.

ABOUT THE AUTHORS

Nancy A. Hewitt (Ph.D., University of Pennsylvania) is Professor Emerita of History and of Women's and Gender Studies at Rutgers University. Her publications include *Southern Discomfort: Women's Activism in Tampa, Florida, 1880s–1920s*, for which she received the Julia Cherry Spruill Prize from the Southern Association of Women Historians; *Women's Activism and Social Change: Rochester, New York, 1822–1872*; and the edited volume *No Permanent Waves: Recasting Histories of U.S. Feminism*. Her latest book—*Radical Friend: Amy Kirby Post and Her Activist Worlds*—appeared in 2018.

Steven F. Lawson (Ph.D., Columbia University) is Professor Emeritus of History at Rutgers University. His research interests include U.S. politics since 1945 and the history of the civil rights movement, with a particular focus on black politics and the interplay between civil rights and political culture in the mid-twentieth century. He is the author of many works including *Running for Freedom: Civil Rights and Black Politics in America since 1941*; *Black Ballots: Voting Rights in the South, 1944–1969*; and *In Pursuit of Power: Southern Blacks and Electoral Politics, 1965–1982*.